Akram Khan's *Rush*
Creative Insights

Akram Khan's *Rush*

Creative Insights

Lorna Sanders

Dance Books
Alton

First published in 2004 by Dance Books Ltd,
The Old Bakery, 4 Lenten Street, Alton, Hampshire GU34 1HG
www.dancebooks.co.uk

Production by Liz Morrell & Patrick Donnelly
Printed by Latimer Trend & Company Ltd

ISBN: 1 85273 103 6

Contents

Introduction – using this book

This book is intended to provide teachers with material and information to support the study of Akram Khan's *Rush* (2000) as part of the AQA GCE AS and A level Dance Specification. It will also be useful to those teaching dance at a range of other levels. A video recording of *Rush*, sponsored by the Arts Council England in 2003, is available from Dance Books.

The tasks in Part 4 aim to provide a variety of ideas, practical and theoretical, for approaching *Rush*. Additional material will need to be collected and this is indicated in the text. Teacher's Notes are used to highlight specific points about the delivery of the tasks. Teachers should use their professional judgment to determine the order of a scheme of work appropriate to their individual circumstances.

A separate bibliography is given for South Asian Dance for ease of reference. It should be noted that spellings are not standardised in these books. Indian words are translated into English in different ways. This book uses one version but others are equally acceptable. Indian terms are translated within the text to assist the reader.

Acknowledgements

I wish to extend heartfelt thanks to Akram Khan, Michael Hulls and Andy Cowton for the generous manner in which they allowed me to interview them for this book. There is little published material in respect of *Rush* because it is a work made early in Akram Khan's career so their willingness to remember everything that they could in answer to my questions is very much appreciated. I also thank Farooq Chaudhry for giving me access to the Akram Khan Company archives and permission to use whatever I needed.

Lorna Sanders MA

Fact Page: *Rush* (2000)

Rush (as a work in progress)

Choreographer:	Akram Khan
Composer:	Andy Cowton
Lighting design:	Ann Joseph
Première:	20th – 22nd July, 2000, Rosas Performance Space, PARTS choreographic project, Brussels
Dancers:	Akram Khan, Rachel Morrow, Gemma Higgingbotham, Moya Michael, Igor Chichko
Duration:	25 minutes
Acknowledgements:	curated by Mathilde Monnier for PARTS further supported by Charleroi Danse

Rush (UK première)

Choreographer:	Akram Khan
Composer:	Andy Cowton
Lighting design:	Michael Hulls
Première:	October 5th, Midlands Arts Centre, Birmingham
Dancers:	Akram Khan, Moya Michael, Gwyn Emberton (later Inn Pang Ooi, who also appears in the video)
Duration:	30 minutes
Acknowledgements:	co-funded by Dance Umbrella, Yorkshire Dance Centre, DanceEast, Birmingham DanceXChange and Sampad

PROGRAMME

Loose in Flight – (Stage Version) 12mins

Choreographer & Performer	Akram Khan
Composer	Angie Atmadjaja
Lighting Design	Akram Khan/Charlotte McClelland
Costume	Akram Khan

A Woking Dance Umbrella commission. New dance territory is being created here, with a driving score by Angie Atmadjaja. Akram blends and merges Kathak with contemporary dance. Using Kathak as the structural base, he continuously breaks out into lyrical passages of contemporary action. The river is crossed back and forth.

Loose in Flight – (Film Version) 5mins

Choreographer & Performer	Akram Khan
Composer	Angie Atmadjaja
Producer	Rosa Rogers
Director	Rachel Davies

A Wark Clements & Co production for Channel 4 Television

Fix – 15mins

Choreographer & Performer	Akram Khan
Composer	Nitin Sawhney
Lighting Design	Michael Hulls
Costume	Akram Khan

In a cascading chain reaction of narrative motion, this explosive new solo work draws its energy from Sufism's whirling dervishes and the search for an innovative, chemical fusion of sound, light and movement.

INTERVAL

Rush – 30 mins

Choreography	Akram Khan
Dancers	Gwyn Emberton, Akram Khan
	Moya Michael
Music	Andy Cowton
Lighting Design	Michael Hulls
Costume	Akram Khan

A purely abstract work inspired by the observation of paragliders in 'freefall'– a physical state between tremendous speed and serene stillness. A rare Indian cycle of nine and a half beats is the choreography's basic structure for movement, space and music.

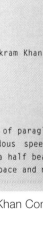

Programme flyer for *Rush*, debut UK tour. Akram Khan Company

Part 1
The Creators

Biographies, characteristics of their work, and the place of Rush *within their careers.*

- *Choreographer: Akram Khan*
- *Selected Choreography of Akram Khan*
- *Summary of the Choreographic Characteristics of Akram Khan*
- *Composer: Andy Cowton*
- *Lighting Designer: Michael Hulls*

Thu 26 - Sat 28 Oct 8pm
LILIAN BAYLIS THEATRE 020 7863 8000
Tickets £10   Concessions £7

COMMISSIONED BY DANCE UMBRELLA

photo: Chris Nash

Akram Khan

"Khan contains both speed and stillness, whirling on his heels, poised between thought and action. A truly astonishing fusion of talents." The Observer

Akram Khan harnesses the quick shifting foot patterns of Kathak dance to the broader sweeping gestures of contemporary dance. He reveals a new dance language that is challenging, beautiful and compelling. Although only in his mid-twenties Khan has already been hailed as a star of the future and in 1999 he was a recipient of a coveted Jerwood Choreography Award.

The programme opens with a screening of the solo, *Loose in Flight*, a film made for Channel 4, in which Khan uses Kathak as the structural base continuously attempting to break out into lyrical passages of contemporary action. Live performances follow - *Fix*, with a specially composed score from **Nitin Sawhney**, and acclaimed by Time Out as "one of the most powerful and compelling solos to hit the stage in years". The programme is completed by *Rush*, inspired by the sensation of watching paragliders in freefall. It features three dancers investigating the notion of falling who shift through space at enormous speed.

Fri 27 Oct
MEET THE ARTIST
Free discussion after the performance

Page from the festival brochure advertising Khan's performances as part of Dance Umbrella 2000.
Akram Khan Company

The Choreographer: Akram Khan

(Expanded from an article written by Lorna Sanders published in *Dancing Times*, May 2003.)

Early dance experience

When writing of Akram Khan critics use superlatives. Khan has: a 'dazzling mixture of macho foot speed and honeyed muscular tone' (Brown 2002); a 'lyrically generous upper body ... commanding, graceful and charismatic, [and] a blistering percussive attack' (Craine 2001). He refers to his career as a 'roller-coaster ride' (Khan 2003).[1]

Akram Khan, of Bangladesh heritage, was born in London in 1974. His mother's interest in dance was key. She introduced him to Bengali folk dancing and when he was seven took him to the celebrated Kathak teacher, Sri Pratap Pawar. Theatre and drama were also influential. His first professional role, touring in *The Adventures of Mowgli*, came when he was ten. As a teenager he spent two years in Peter Brooks' play, *The Mahabharata*. Khan's A levels included Bengali and (significantly) mathematics. Khan states Kathak has a 'geometric ... mathematical precision' (Bragg 2002). He also continued his dance studies as Pawar's disciple, being formally presented by him in his first solo recital at eighteen (Willis 2001). The guru-disciple relationship is special. As Ravi Shankar explains, the student learns 'all the process of life which relates to the art form also' (Bragg 2002). Khan admires Pawar's 'masculine yet graceful style' and clearly embodies this ideal (Khan 2000b).

Khan's mother encouraged him towards a dance degree and in 1994 he went to De Montfort University. It was his first experience of ballet and contemporary dance. His mother had taken him to the ballet as a small child but, having also been to the film *Gandhi*, he 'fell asleep in the comfortable seats'. His first contemporary class at De Montfort left him perplexed so he watched a video of DV8's *Strange Fish*; 'I was shocked — but in a positive way. I thought it fascinating'. After two years he went to the Northern School of Contemporary Dance and graduated with the highest marks ever awarded. Thus he added classical ballet, Graham, Cunningham, Alexander, release-based techniques, contact improvisation and physical theatre to his dance experiences.

---

[1] Unless indicated further quotations by Khan are from this source.

Loose in Flight (1995)

In 1995 he choreographed the solo *Loose in Flight* experimenting with 'loosening the bolts' of Kathak's rules (Bragg 2002). Descriptions highlight the dual attractions of Khan's powerful stage presence and emerging style. For example: 'he is extraordinarily present in performance... his... arms define distances like Blake's drawing of God measuring the universe' (Parry 2001); 'tension exploding into... liquid eloquence... is balanced by... cool aplomb' (Hale 2002). The movement, initiated by various joints, was embellished with small flicks of the head and athletic Eurocrash-style rolls.[2] A programme note states; 'Kathak [is] the structural base, he continuously breaks out into lyrical passages of contemporary action. The river is crossed back and forth' (Anonymous 2000a). This final metaphor hints at two separate strands (Kathak and Contemporary) within the solo. Khan explains now that he was trying tested models and needed a choreographic process that opened up the possibilities for a more distinctive creativity of his own. He found this in 1999 working with Jonathan Burrows on *Duet*. This gave insight into 'how much deeper you can cut below the surface, then you realise where you'd like to explore further'.

Fix (1995)

Khan made *Fix* with a Jerwood Choreography Award using a 'myriad of ideas' (Khan 2000b); Whirling Devishes and the connections to Kathak spins, ideas of continuous energy and spatial restriction, how energy flows outwards from the core to the extremities but instead of being dissipated it rebounds back in again. Burrows helped with advice. Hints of body popping and robotics from break dancing occur in the disruptions of flow (as a child Khan admired Michael Jackson). Key interests are evident: improvisation from a Kathak base; a highly theatrical product; and collaborative working. Sawhney's music echoes with temple/cathedral, mediaeval, ritualistic and contemporary qualities. Michael Hulls' overlapping oblongs illuminate the floor in soft focus. Movement is complex: an arm sticks out dislocated, resistant to jerky pulls; Khan, Marcel Marceau-like, inches past his own elbow joint which appears stuck in the space.[3] Gestures fail to hold and flash in serpentine trajectories; dance is in hyper-speed but with no loss of clarity. On exit Khan

---

[2] Dance critics invented the term to describe the style favoured by certain European choreographers. It involves a full-blooded diving or crashing onto the floor.

[3] Marcel Marceau – famous French mime artist.

plucks a near-invisible string and a puff of talc leaves an ambient trace behind. The dance is both fixed and transient simultaneously. An abstract approach is indicated; Khan stated 'they [the audience] are free … to have a view on it, whatever it may be' (Khan 2000b).

Fix was programmed with traditional Kathak material which Khan now keeps separate. He explains: 'I have to close off from the contemporary for a time and become an 'Indian' again, I have to think like a Kathak dancer, the aesthetic has to be transferred and a mental adjustment made'. This indicates an intense preparation period and living the part like an actor preparing a role. Khan is a perfectionist (befitting a classical dancer). In *Polaroid Feet* (2000), an evening of traditional Kathak, 'he achieves … precise physical detail preserved within a blur of speed … Khan's upper body … [is] the key to his uniqueness. His torso has a strength and elasticity that allow him to arch, dip and spiral with extravagant grace' (Mackrell 2001).

Rush (2000)

A Lisa Ullmann Travelling Scholarship took Khan to Anne Teresa de Keersmaeker's PARTS school in Brussels to participate in the X group project for six months, a choreographic platform for young choreographers to develop their own movement language.[4] He states; I was able to 'investigate my interests on other peoples' bodies more. This was different from doing it the way I was taught, it could be a real experimentation to find my own way.' Here he experimented with material for *Rush* (2000) using four dancers in addition to himself. Kathak is traditionally a solo performance so this was significant. *Rush* was pivotal in establishing his own company and allowed Khan to make the transition from being a solo performer. Some critics said they could not take their eyes from him but the 'question of whether Khan can transfer his skills to other bodies is part-answered by *Rush* … at first, you watch only him, then the structure takes over' (Parry 2000). Such comments continue and Khan admits to finding this frustrating. Other choreographers with idiosyncratic perform-ance styles (Wayne McGregor and Russell Maliphant for example) have been similarly received, as if uniqueness needed justification by exact duplication. Khan's company achieved quick success, appearing at prestigious international dance festivals.

---

[4] PARTS – Performing Arts Research Training Studios.

Front page of theatre programme for Brussel's première of *Rush*. Akram Khan Company

A unique style: Contemporary Kathak

In 2000 Khan received a *Time Out* Live award and was nominated Outstanding Newcomer by the Critics Circle for his 'unique style' (Anonymous 2000b). Critics came up with the term Contemporary Kathak and Khan uses this still; 'for clarity you should provide a reference point for the audience – but I'm not deep enough into the work yet to know what to call it'. His interests lie in investigating the language of movement. He traces the antecedents of this; an alien style, Contemporary Dance, was imposed and led to confusion in the muscles. Jonathan Burrows helped to clarify his thinking, having pointed to the mixing of information in the body. So is it a new language? 'For me it is', Khan replies. He dislikes the term fusion, 'it implies lack of force, deliberation and depth'. His style 'was not an intellectual decision, it was organic' with the subconscious mixing of the learning processes of Kathak and Contemporary.

Khan explains that 'teaching is an important part of learning'. Pawar advised him to teach beginners because it allows a re-examination of your beliefs. For the past four years Khan has taken a group of 6-7 year olds for Kathak on Sundays, an advanced student taking over when he cannot be there. Khan also teaches workshops for professionals. Explaining to others helps with clarification. He notes: 'fast isn't fast enough, it is all relative, speed is a technique of itself and people have a natural tempo – push them past that boundary and they can't control it. Fast and fluid is my aim.'

Related Rocks (2001)

Khan was commissioned by the London Sinfonietta to create *Related Rocks* (2001) and continued his interest in making group pieces. Kathak concepts and abstract interests are key; beginning and ending with a lone dancer, the group moved to the sound of Lindberg's voice. 'Tersely angled gestures ... sliced ... through the clipped cadences ... by the time the first note sounded we were ... primed to read the dancing less as an emotional response to the music than as a powerful rhythmic argument with it' (Mackrell 2001). Khan had typically explored non-narrative structures and formal qualities but critics detected a new element; 'flashes of mutual acknowledgement among the performers' (Hale 2002). The theme hinted at a more allusive approach, 'Lindberg's piece was based on the destruction and construction of a piano, so I immediately thought of Shiva as the creator and destroyer, and we used all the gestures of Shiva ...[it was a] test run for *Kaash*' (Anonymous 2002b).

In 2001 Khan became Choreographer in Residence at the Royal Festival Hall. He also acted in Peter Brook's film, *Hamlet* and undertook a fourteen months overseas and UK tour. Khan is grateful for the support he gets from the UK and Europe, such as the Théâtre de la Ville in Paris and Vooruit in Ghent. 'They are not looking for work out of the multicultural box, they see my work as contemporary and of the moment – they fly over to see it before they programme it so you know it is because they appreciate it'. It is important not to be pigeon-holed and he resists the need to conform to other people's agendas. A unique viewpoint is vital. He does not like work that is a 'copy of a copy of a copy – there has to be something that is YOU, that is honest'.

Khan's first full length work: *Kaash* (2002)

Kaash (2002) was Khan's first full length work. Starting points included the 'symbolism of traditional Indian Gods [as] representations of rhythmical patterns and specific movement qualities' (Anonymous 2002a).[5] There are no overt references (a focus on rhythm and dynamic qualities is indicated) but Śiva's cyclical creation-destruction aspect is inherent. (See Appendix 1). The choreographic structure 'adopts the cinematic idea of flashback where the end is seen at the beginning and then unravels to reveal how it arrived at its conclusion' (Anonymous 2002a). Thus a meditative middle section is sandwiched between two energetic eruptions in which the 'dance pattern splinters and coheres ... [the dancers] following different time cycles.' (Parry 2002). Sawhney mentions the notion of multiple, parallel universes in Western physics; 'a multiverse'(Anonymous 2002c).

Khan's reputation allowed an ambitious collaboration with the internationally renowned artist/sculptor, Anish Kapoor. Kapoor explains; 'collage in any art form is of no interest. The idea that two entities independent of each other can come together somewhere in the middle... is not something I believe in... what I see in Akram is the possibility of coming out of that tradition and inventing something completely different'(Frater 2002). Kapoor provided a void, a minimalist 'dense black square painted on gauze that vibrates like a hungry hole, poised to suck in any passing matter' (Mackrell 2002c). The piece again opens with a lone dancer. He gazes into the blackness and a woman enters and whispers to him. (Hints of Parvati and Śiva perhaps?) A cataclysm of cosmic proportions ensues. The dancers form war-like columns from which they break out, arms slicing with an energy that would split atoms.

[5] The elephant headed Ganesha was associated with swinging actions and 3 beats for example, while the destroyer Śiva has 7 beats and highly vigorous qualities.

Related Rocks links to interests that Khan went on to explore in *Kaash*; one work often provides a thread and even movement material that he continues to explore in another (like *Fix* and *Rush*, see Part 3), indeed he continues to refine and rework pieces as they tour. *Kaash* changed over time. Khan explains how the movement begins to bed down in the muscles and then

> I become fascinated by boredom in the body, which becomes creative again as the body reacts against this. Kaash is more of a quintet now, the meditative 'reflection' section is developed and there are more solos so we can develop what it means more. First there is an instinctive working, then a break in the tour gives you time to be analytical again. (Khan 2004)

Use of Music

Music is significant and Khan approaches it differently for each piece; 'though you can't avoid there being a signature'. Minimalism and complexity are intricately related for Khan. 'I want to argue with the music, go within it and without it, to speak to it rather than merely go with it.' This implies a predilection for complexity but he speaks of the significance of contrasts. The use of simplicity or clarity in the body controlling the chaotic, complex energy of Kathak for example; 'can you translate something simple into complexity and what happens to it then? And vice versa – intriguing'. Khan used to provide his dancers with material but now gives them tasks. For *Kaash* the dancers improvised with the rhythmic forms and qualities of Khan's Kathak performance earlier that year at the Purcell Room. His role, although more directorial now, is to find 'a single vision'. He acknowledges it has been difficult to find suitable dancers. He explains; 'for the time being I wouldn't use Kathak dancers simply because I feel that classical dancers have a boundary... it took a lot of training ... to be able to move past that... at this present time I don't have that amount of time to train' (Khan 2002).

Red or White (2003)

His piece *Red or White* (2003) for George Piper Dances was based on the format of a playful question and answer session between himself and them (the idea coming from an interview in Monaco which included a quick fire session with no thinking time). He gave them a Kathak class and asked them to improvise in order to find comfortable material.[6] Khan sums up; 'so you ask questions and expect certain answers – but then you don't get the question

[6] *Red or White* was a trio for Matthew Hart, William Trevitt and Michael Nunn.

you thought you wanted or the answer you expected. Indeed there are questions with no answers'.

Associate Artist at the Royal Festival Hall and *Ma* (2004)

In April 2003 Khan was made Associate Artist at the Royal Festival Hall (a two-year appointment), the first time this status has been afforded to a non-musician. This involved making a trilogy of Kathak performances based on the male Hindu gods (the third part is planned for spring 2005) and, in collaboration with the writer Hanif Kureishi, *A God of Small Tales* for a group of mature women. The title indicates a burgeoning narrative interest. He asked the dancers to draw on their memories of childhood to create movement. In the brief interview included on the video of *Rush* Khan lists a host of influences on his work in general. The continuing importance of film is indicated by Khan's desire to create a sense of 'patience' in *A God of Small Tales* like the slow journey of the protagonist in David Lynch's film of 1999, *The Straight Story*, who travels across the USA on a lawn mower to visit his dying brother (Khan 2004).

A God of Small Tales provided a background experience that connects to his new work *Ma* (mother, mother earth, nature), his second full-length piece for a bigger company of seven dancers. A student on work placement from the Northern School of Contemporary Dance is to dance his role during the choreographic process to allow Khan to stand outside and evaluate the whole stage picture; an important step with a larger group. He is planning to abandon his typical black and white costumes and is looking at a strong orange-yellow instead, having been influenced by the colours in the film *Kill Bill*. The opportunity to revisit *Kaash* and its themes of destruction means that a reworked solo from it is being taken as one of the starting points for *Ma*, which also involves text from Hanif Kureishi and dramaturgy from Carmen Mehnert.[7] On his company website Khan provides a series of questions as inspirations; 'where is earth if it has everybody to build on it... where is earth if it has nobody to nurture it? Where is earth if it has nobody to water it... where is earth if it has nobody to witness it?' This all indicates a stronger sense of narrative investigation beginning to re-emerge. The term re-emerge is chosen because classical Kathak performance involves both abstract and narrative aspects but Khan now appears ready to explore this aspect anew in his group work. *Ma* is about human relationships because different starting points lead to different aspects of movement; 'I've just touched the skin, I can still go deeper'.

[7] A collaborator with Alain Platel's Belgium company, Les Ballets C de la B.

In 2005 Khan will create a duet with the choreographer/performer Sidi Larbi, who is perhaps best known in the UK for his work with Alain Platel's company of actor/dancers Les Ballets C de la B whose work includes *Rein de Rein* (1999) and *Foi* (2003). Larbi's work is challenging and richly resonant in narrative content. Khan's inspiration for the duet is again influenced by film. He admires the fast-paced, interlocking martial arts choreography in the recent films, *Crouching Tiger Hidden Dragon* and *The Matrix*. The warrior is a theme Khan has explored before. Inspired by Arjuna from the Hindu epic *Māhabhārata*, *Ronin* (2003) was 'based on an exploration of the conversation he has with Krishna when he's preparing for battle, about what he feels is immoral and moral, what is just and unjust' (Anonymous 2003a).[8] Khan's acting experience continues to be significant in many ways. He explains, 'I see in scenes – the images evolve until they seem to come to an end and overlap into the next scene. The more I make work, the more I learn how I work and I work cinematically' (Khan 2004).

In 2004 Khan received an Honorary Doctorate of Arts from De Montfort University for his 'innovative contribution to the development of dance in the UK'.

[8] The term Ronin means warrior.

Selected Choreography of Akram Khan

(Abbreviation: m. music; l. lighting; c. costume; d. set design)

Date	Title	Music/design/lighting	Company/notes
1995	*Loose in Flight*	m: Angie Atmadjaja; l: Akram Khan/Charlotte McClelland; c: Akram Khan	Première: Vooriut Geliud Festival, Belgium; UK première: Woking Dance Umbrella. Solo for Khan
1999	*Loose in Flight*		Première: October, Channel 4 TV; director: Rachel Davies. Film version. Extract available on CD-ROM produced by Kadam, *Living Tradition* (2000)
	Desert Steps	m: Kevin Volans	Duet with Jonathan Burrows
	Fix	m: Nitin Sawhney; l: Michael Hulls; c: Akram Khan	See note.[9] Première: Tron Theatre, Glasgow, New Moves Festival 2000. Solo for Khan. Available on video, Spring ReLoaded 6
2000	*Rush*	m: Andy Cowton; l: Michael Hulls; c: Akram Khan	Première: as a work in progress, Brussels, with lights by Ann Joseph; UK première: Midland Arts Centre, Birmingham. Akram Khan Company
2001	*Polaroid Feet*	m: tabla played by Vishnu Sahai	See note.[10] Première: Purcell Room, Royal Festival Hall, London. Solo Kathak programme, included pieces by Pratap Pawar and Gauri Sharma Tripati
	Related Rocks	m: Magnus Lindberg; l: Aideen Malone; c: Saeunn Huld	Première: Queen Elizabeth Hall, Royal Festival Hall, London. Akram Khan Company
2002	*Kaash*	m: Nitin Sawhney; d: Anish Kapoor; l: Aideen Malone	Première: Queen Elizabeth Hall, Royal Festival Hall, London. Akram Khan Company
2003	*Red or White*	m: mukul; l: Aideen Malone	Première: Queen Elizabeth Hall, Royal Festival Hall, London. George Piper Dances

[9] It is usual to date works by their world première rather than when they were created. Numerous sources list *Fix* as 1999, in order not to cause confusion it is listed as such here although it was not premièred until 2000.

[10] The date for this work is incorrectly given in several places as 2000. It was however his inaugural performance when he was became choreographer in residence at the Royal Festival Hall in 2001.

Date	Title	Music/design/lighting	Company/notes
20003	*Ronin*	tabla played by Partha Sarathi Mukherjee; text: Hanif Kureishi	Première: Purcell Room, Royal Festival Hall, London. Solo Kathak programme, included pieces by Pratap Pawar
2004	*A God of Small Tales*	text: Hanif Kureishi; m: Faheem Mazhar, Philip Sheppard	Première: Queen Elizabeth Hall, Royal Festival Hall, London. Commissioned by Royal Festival Hall Education
	Ma	m: Riccardo Nova; l: Mikki Kunttu; text: Hanif Kureishi	Première: Victoria Theatre, Singapore. UK première: Edinburh Festival. Akram Khan Company

Documentary

South Bank Show, ITV, October 2002 (includes extracts from *Kaash*)

Summary of the Choreographic Characteristics of Akram Khan

- Contemporary Kathak.
- Interest in exploration of energy routes through the body and effects of this.
- Strong gestural interest in torso and arms.
- Feet propel, travel, support, some use of gesture – though less decorative than arms.
- Speed as a technique in, and of, itself.
- Linear formations – columns, frieze forms, tableaux, diagonals.
- Complex structural relationships to produce visual rhythmic interest.
- Repetition, reordering, recombining, accumulation of variations.
- Dancers share similar material – attention is not drawn to gender differences.
- Filmic treatment – cutting/splicing material together, episodic phrases.
- Increasing use of improvisation and chance-based operations.
- Theatrical presentation (though minimal physical setting) and collaborative approach.
- Interest is in formal qualities of movement.
- Abstract treatment of themes but an increasing allusiveness and interest in narrative.
- Revisiting/reworking themes and material – one work feeds into and links with another.
- Juxtaposition of simplicity and complexity – minimalism and embellishment.

Composer: Andy Cowton

Although chance played a part in Andy Cowton becoming a composer, his interest in music stretches back to childhood. He learned to play the trumpet and sang in a church choir from age eight to sixteen which taught him the fundamentals of choral music: melody; harmony; and structure; 'it was treated very seriously, we did a Passion every year and met twice, and sometimes three times a week for rehearsal' (Sanders 2004a).[11] During his sixth form years he also became interested in drama when Al Dicks, who taught the subject at Bradford University, introduced lunchtime workshops at his school; 'his enthusiasm was infectious and I loved doing it'. By chance he saw an article about Dartington College of Arts[12] in a Sunday newspaper supplement and it caught his imagination. 'It looked like an outward bound course, students were swinging from the trees'. He joined their Theatre Language course and studied contact improvisation and dance with Mary Fulkerson and Rosemary Butcher.[13] He also had the opportunity to play Gamelan music and was drawn to the unusual percussion instruments.[14] Cowton continued to pursue an interest in movement. He toured with Fulkerson's dance group, joined Ava Lundquist's company for a year, as a trainee and performer in Stockholm and worked freelance on returning to London, including performing with Yolande Snaith's company.

Living off his wits and experimenting with synthesised music

During the mid 1980s Cowton also studied electronic music at Morley College in London, taught by Barry Anderson. He had been experimenting with simple four-track tape recoding and wanted access to more sophisticated machinery; 'using synthesised sound as a possible source of music was great for someone not trained formally in music composition'. He used collage techniques and sampling processes to create soundscapes. 'You find some interesting sound textures from a range of different materials and layer them up using tape loops. I did it just because I was loving it.' In particular he became interested in metal as a source of unusual noise. Finding sound and making eclectic collections appealed; Cowton recalls his own amazement at Jean Tingulay's ability to collect disparate objects into his sculp-

---

[11] All subsequent quotations are from this source.

[12] Dartington College in Devon is a long established alternative/experimental institution. It embraced post modern dance in the 1970s.

[13] For further details of Butcher's work see Stephanie Jordan's *Striding Out*, (Dance Books, 1992).

[14] Indonesian music using a wide range of string, woodwind and percussion instruments.

tures, 'this was a big influence on me'. At this period 'living off your wits' also became essential. He undertook life-modelling for art classes to earn money. Motion was required for this rather than still positions and he produced a score for a performance installation at the eventual exhibition of the artwork that was produced. He also joined Test Department, an agitprop band who used scrap metal as percussion instruments.

A career as a composer develops

Percussion was an enduring interest. At the Laban Centre he played drums to accompany contemporary dance classes, teaching himself how to play them.[15] Here he met Duncan MacFarland, the teacher of the class. They began a three year collaboration which started with *Albert's Dream*, for which he sampled vocal records of Hildegaard of Bingen before she was familiar to the wider public. Cowton's typical approach is to make non-acoustic, non-tonal work that does not require live performance; 'I tamper with sounds'. Eventually he began to create pieces for Russell Maliphant, of which the first was *Unspoken* (1996). Although Michael Hulls, the lighting designer, had graduated before Cowton the Dartington connection provided a like-minded collaboration. Movement is usually the starting point but lighting played its part in the collaborative process and typically chance also played a hand in finding sound. At one point an aeroplane resonated round the rehearsal building so Cowton built this sensation into the sound track. Critics noted that the accompaniment evoked an allusive atmosphere that enhanced the movement. It

> summons a variety of unspecifically hostile environments. A lost-in-space reverberation is cut by sparse electronic blips and a hospital soundscape is the background for what seems like a series of glimpses into cubicles or cells. (Jays 1996, p.853)

The emotional effect of the use of sampling is also noted as 'anguish and foreboding creeps in with a voice repeating, 'Dr Kravitz, you have a visitor in the main lobby' (Smith 1998, p.100). A productive collaboration with Maliphant and Hulls followed, including *Two* (1998) and *Liquid Reflex* (1999). They also created *Re-Coil* (1995) for Ricochet Dance Company. For this piece 'nightmare noises, phones and footsteps fade in and out, punctuated by machine-gun ferocity. Opening with a figure ... twitching in her sleep' (Jays 1995, p.895). The selection of found sound again demonstrates how Cowton enhances the emotional quality in Maliphant's abstract yet allusive movement.

---

[15] The Laban Centre offers BA degrees in dance.

Rush (2000): a collaborative process

Cowton met Akram Khan through the connection with Maliphant and Hulls and was commissioned to compose the accompaniment for *Rush*. He was able to go to Brussels and saw some of the early ideas for the dance material. As with Hulls the aim was to support the movement. Collaboration is important because Cowton does not compose music for its own sake, 'I don't write music for myself. I try to get the right feeling in the first place and then when it comes together it isn't really chance at all'.

Video Installations

Cowton's music has been used by other choreographers including Fin Walker, Shobana Jeyasingh, Mark Murphy and Wayne McGregor. He composes for television documentaries and for film. He has continued to make sound scores for installations. In 2001 he collaborated with Hulls on *Shadowspace*, a light and video piece with dancer Anna Williams. He has also provided music for split screen installations in gallery spaces with the visual artist, Isaac Julien: in 1999 they collaborated on *Three*, a dance film with Bebe Miller and Ralph Lemmen; in 2000 on *The Long Road to Mazatlan* which was Turner Prize nominated; and in 2003 *Baltimore* was premiered at the newly opened FACT Centre for Film, Art and Creative Technology in Liverpool. Maliphant is also recreating *Two* for Sylvie Guillem so Cowton's music may reach a more traditional dance audience.

Lighting Designer: Michael Hulls

Early interests in set and costume design

Michael Hulls is one of the key British lighting designers who have reinvigorated this aspect of production, moving it into the realm of art rather than craft. He is particularly known for his collaborations with the choreographer, Russell Maliphant where lighting is developed as an equal partner in the creative process and can even be the starting point.[16] At age 14 Hulls joined a youth theatre group and although he enjoyed performing, his chief interest was in set design. He describes himself 'as a design-based, life form'.[17] He came into contact with 'the mysteries of the cables and lamps' at this point too, holding the ladder while a friend set up the lighting for their productions. Sets and costumes seemed the first choice for him and he looked for a BA course to continue this study. Youth theatre was important in giving him experience but it did not involve 'understanding, I realised that I needed a broader education in theatre'.

In the 1970s there were only few courses of this type. He went for interviews but after the practical engagement of his earlier experiences it 'seemed rather dry to be asked to produce designs and models that were not going to happen'. His father saw an advertisement for a BA course at Dartington College of Arts that involved theatre and dance. On enquiring what his father knew of the place Hulls discovered that his aunt had studied painting there in the 1940s. It was an open and exciting place that encouraged great personal freedom and suited him. He was also the only person in his year with experience of lighting so he lit his own and friends' work.

First professional lighting commission

After graduation Hulls joined others from the theatre and art departments and formed a performance company to create site-specific work. They lived in derelict buildings 'to get a real feel for the place and draw ideas from it, real site-specific work not just alternative venues, unlike some of the pieces around at that time'. He then spent some time as a freelance set and costume designer but did not find this a satisfying experience. Laurie Booth

---

[16] See (Sanders 2002) for an analysis of the work of the dancer/choreographer Russell Maliphant.
[17] Unless otherwise indicated all quotation of Hulls refers to (Sanders 2004b).

provided the answer. Hulls had already met him while studying at Dartington where Booth, dancer/choreographer and ex graduate, returned to visit the college from time to time. He asked Hulls to light his new piece, *Spatial Decay II* (1990) a duet for Booth and Russell Maliphant. Unusually, like the movement, the lighting was to be improvised, 'it wasn't scary because I didn't know any better... because I didn't have any ideas about it, there was complete freedom' (Hutera, 2004). Booth felt he could trust Hulls because of their shared background and training at Dartington. For example, both had been taught contact im-provisation by Steve Paxton and Mary Fulkerson.[18] After a performance of *Spatial Decay II* at Riverside Studios in London Hulls was offered an Arts Council Bursary to study lighting. It seemed important to capitalise on this fresh approach to lighting being displayed.

Jennifer Tipton's Workshop

Hulls used his bursary to attend Jennifer Tipton's two-week workshop for choreographers and lighting designers in New York. He already knew of her work, where light is an equal partner to movement, through Booth. Tipton had 'become the preferred lighting designer of half of the USA's choreographers' (De Marigny 1993/94, p.12). What did she teach him? Hulls answers; 'how good her eyes were. You have to see better because that is your tool. There must be sensitivity in the way that you look. And it was reassurance that the way that I wanted to work wasn't off the map. Dana Reitz and Jennifer work in equal partnership and I wanted to work in that way'.[19]

A long-term collaboration with Russell Maliphant

After returning to the UK Hulls continued to light for Booth but began to collaborate with Maliphant on a regular basis. 'Russell had an incredible sensitivity to light, placing himself carefully, knowing where he was in relation to it and seeming to understand the effect of this on the visibility of the movement and the type of movement therefore to create'. Maliphant

[18] Steve Paxton pioneered contact improvisation in the USA and was a seminal figure in the development of post modern dance. Contact improvisation uses all surfaces of the body to support, or give weight to, a partner. It relies on trust and momentum and is used widely by contemporary and post modern choreographers.

[19] Reitz is a post modern dancer/choreographer working in the USA.

also attended one of Tipton's workshops in London in 1993. Another participant stated that it provided

> a liberation ... finding a way to talk about lighting dance, not in the borrowed language of theatre, in terms of location or atmosphere, but in a complimentary language of structure, shape and texture. (Burrows 1994, p29).

This review of the London course clarifies the attraction of Tipton's approach. Hulls works in a similar manner. Indeed Maliphant states that 'with Mike the architecture of the space is always changing, opening up or closing down' (Hutera, 2004).

Hulls' long-term collaboration with Maliphant on the interaction between light and movement began with *Unspoken* (1996). Maliphant explains; 'we wanted to reverse a more regular approach where ... light is put on at the end ... Michael designed and set up a rig and we began to work with that over several weeks' (Brannigan, 2001). Lighting thus becomes an integral part of the creative process and produces some magical effects,

> the arcing limb leaves behind it a blurred image in a trace pathway, rather like the after image created by a hand held firework in the dark .... a real dancing body, existing in real time and space, denies its corporeality and temporarily becomes a living evocation of a photograph using time-lapse exposure. (Sanders 2002, p.53).

Akram Khan's *Fix* (1999)

Hulls also regularly lit Jonathan Burrow's work and first met Akram Khan when Khan performed *Duet* with Burrows in 1999. Khan wanted Hulls to light his solo *Fix* (1999). He was to be away in Brussels at that point so there were practical problems to solve. Only a minimal amount of time together was possible though Hulls prefers to work in an inter-dependent, collaborative way. With Burrows 'the movement and light were independent, each having its own rhythm and pattern. So it had to be this way for Akram too'. He designed the lights before *Fix* was made to allow Khan to be placed anywhere in the space, overlapping blue and white oblongs providing a chequer-board effect floor. Hulls' choice of colour is typically both practical and evocative. 'Blue is the closest to painting a floor black, if it has white marks it makes them invisible and the floor looks really black, darkness made visible. Blue also suggests infinity, depth and shadow. Shadows in natural light are bluish. Without blue the space can look stark, so it also softens this.'

Hulls also likes to create a non-specific space that structures territory. The lights for *Fix* create their own pattern and rhythm but being rectangular they are also appropriate to Khan's angular movement and linear floor patterns. They are sympathetic to the music too. 'I am not there to compete but to support the dance and provide a visual framework that allows people's imaginations to take them where they will.' As with the dance, Khan stated 'they [the audience] are free... to have a view on it, whatever it may be', the aim of the lighting is not to close down options but to create an abstract world in which the dance can operate (2000b). This however also shapes the decisions that follow so there is a consistency; 'it determines what other lighting effects can be used, it's not just a mishmash'.

Light also evokes mood and affects the way that the audience perceives energy. 'There is a psychological response to light, for example, in dim light everyone talks more quietly. Light is energy and one of the uses of light is to define space and time which do not exist without energy – it is about the amount of energy put into a space.'

Akram Khan's *Rush* (2000)

Khan also asked Hulls to provide the lighting for *Rush* but because of work commitments he could not get to Brussels, where it was to première as a work in progress. He designed *Rush* after the first showing; 'I had hoped for a clean sheet but perhaps this was naïve'. Ann Joseph provided the original lights for the Brussels première and it was 'perhaps inevitable that these would become part of the language of the piece and have to be taken into account, Akram became attached to certain moments he couldn't detach himself from, which made it more difficult because the dance had become something already, it had an identity'. Hulls is a perfectionist; 'it was a struggle and I am still not satisfied with it totally'.

Hulls brought in Aideen Malone to take care of the lighting for the tour and to look after his work. She studied at Trinity College Dublin and at Goldsmiths College London, and has also lit for theatre and opera. She has now been a regular collaborator creating the lighting design for *Polaroid Feet* (2000), *Related Rocks* (2001) and *Kaash* (2002).

Hulls has now led workshops with Maliphant around the world and in 2002 they won a *Time Out* Award for Outstanding Collaboration for *Sheer* (2001). Hulls first worked for George Piper Dances in 2001 when Maliphant restaged *Critical Mass* (1998) for them. For this company he also lit Christopher Wheeldon's *Mesmerics* (2003) and all of Maliphant's works, including *Torsion* (2002). In 2003, for the Royal Ballet, he lit Maliphant's *Broken Fall*, danced by Sylvie Guillem, Michael Nunn and William Trevitt.

Part 2
Background Context

Kathak
* *A brief history of the development of the style*
* *An introduction to the technique, music and costume*
* *South Asian and Contemporary Dance in the UK*
* *Bibliography and Resources for South Asian Dance*
* *Websites for key organisations supporting South Asian Arts*
* *Key Visual Resources*

Kathak: a brief history of the development of the style

A word about classicism

This is not the classicism of the narrow Euro-Centric model of Greek and Roman antiquity. It establishes its own identity within the history of Indian dance: it conforms to a prescribed set of principles; it establishes an ideal and an aesthetic of the body; it values technical virtuosity; it uses a frontal orientation, an upright posture and effortlessness; it has an internal logic with expressive qualities that are allusive rather than explicitly literal; it uses a formal etiquette in its presentation; it has a range of codified steps; and has an inter-dependent and complex relationship with music.

Introduction and some problems

The development of Kathak in what was the north of India (an area that now includes Pakistan and Bangladesh) involves peoples of two religions. Hinduism became established around the 4th century AD. The prophet Muhammad founded the Muslim faith in Arabia in the 7th century AD.

Kathaka is the Sanskrit word for a storyteller.[20] Kathak is one of several classical dance styles that developed in India.[21] Scholars do not agree on the details but generally accept that this classical tradition has evolved from ancient origins. Some scholars point to continuities and similarities in its history while others highlight adaptations and changes through time; 'what is danced now is not at all what was danced two thousand years ago' (Iyer 1997, p.5). The relationship of the present to the past is difficult to assess and only an introduction is possible here. The *Bibliography and Resources* section at the end of Part 2 provides further sources of information. Numerous Sanskrit manuscripts, recording mythic or divine origins for dance, indicate the importance of dance over time in India. Bose (1991) divides the development of Indian classical dance helpfully into three periods.

---

[20] Sanskrit (the ancient, sacred Hindu language) is one of the oldest Indo-European languages.
[21] Other styles include Bharata Natyam, Kathakali, Manipuri, and Odissi. Some scholars now also include Mohini Attam, Kuchpdi and Chhau. See (Iyer 1997).

Period One – the Nātyaśāstra

The first period begins with the writing of the Nātyaśāstra sometime between the 2nd century BC and 4th Century AD (the actual date is uncertain). The sage, Bharata Muni, is traditionally accepted as the author. It dealt with all aspects of theatrical production; drama, dance, music, related arts and crafts, aesthetic principles and philosophy. The art form it described was then already fully established. The book was considered a sacred text or Veda (its contents believed handed down by the gods, see Appendix 1) and not merely a manual of technical aspects although it contained exhaustive detail for all aspects of theatrical production. One chapter dealt with dance and classified movement into two aspects. Nŗitta (nŗtta) 'visualises and reproduces music and rhythms by means of abstract gestures of the body and hands and by extensive and precise use of footwork' (Massey 1989, p.xv) and nritya (nŗtya), story telling, conveys feelings and moods through facial expressions and gestures. Dance was integral to drama, being valued for its ability to add beauty and to praise the gods. Abstract or nŗtta aspects were thus important, however beauty was not for mere decorative effect. It was prized because it drew both spectator and performer into an absorbing aesthetic contemplation, seen as akin to religious experience. [22]

> Dance... an image of the activity of God... identified beauty with the infinite glory of God; and so the expression of beauty has been religious in nature... and thus became an essential part of the worship of the deity. (Banerji 1982, p.8)

The dance technique was codified into 108 karanas (fundamental units of movement comprising posture, hand and leg gestures) that were combined to make angaharas (longer sequences). These karanas, based on Śiva's cosmic dance (see Appendix 1) are preserved in stone panels adorning the walls of various temples, including the Temple of Natārāja at Chidambaram in South India. The Nātyaśāstra does not mention temple dancing but at some point the devadāsī, the hereditary caste of female temple dancers, were established to perform the karanas. As the knowledge contained within the śāstra was considered divine revelation the framework it set down was adhered to. It became developed in subsequent texts and manuscripts written over the centuries. A tradition also emerged at some point for storytellers to enact the epic stories of the gods from the Rāmayāna (written around the 2nd to 3rd century AD) and the Mahābharāta (written around the 4th century AD).

---

[22] See (Coomaraswamy 1985) for a full exposition of the concept of rasa or aesthetic emotion.

An evening's entertainment: Akbar the Great on a terrace with female dancers and musicians.

Period Two – dance develops independence from drama

In the second period, the 11th to 15th centuries, dance and music became increasingly inter-related and gained independence from drama. New regional styles (categorised as desī in the growing śāstra literature) emerged in addition to the now older (margī) Bharata tradition described in the Nātyaśāstra, though scholars believe these represent different stylistic approaches rather than widely divergent forms. For example, margī was 'sacred to the gods and danced for them ... [desī was for] the pleasure of humans' (Massey 1989, p.xiii).[23] The division of dance into nṛtta and nṛtya (abstract and story telling) was fully established, indeed forms today still adhere to this, but nātya aspects in dance also developed further and became incorporated as abhinaya (dance-drama and mimetic elements).

The devadāsī dancers thrived. The cult of Krishna influenced medieval Indian art, Krishna's romantic love for Rādhā symbolising the love of God for Man. It provided new religious themes and stories that infused dance via the songs that often accompanied it. The sacred Ras Lila plays from the Braj area also popularised the Rādhā-Krishna stories. These may also have introduced a stronger element of story telling to dance; 'professional narrators who were attached to temples ... were known as Kathakars' at this point (Khokar 1988, p.47). The growth of different devotional cults in this period resulted in the spread of temples, which along with the Hindu courts provided a large patronage for the arts. The dancing at court, although for entertainment, was not entirely separate from its religious function because 'the patron of both temple and court was the ruler... seen, in Hindu India, as the representative on earth of the divinity' (Iyer 1997. p.7).

Period Three – from temple to court and the origins of Kathak

In the 16th to 19th centuries, during the Moghul Empire in North India, Kathak began to emerge as a separate style. More specifically the third period began in 1526, when the Persians invaded. It continued until 1857, when the British took control of the region.[24] The *Nartananirnaya*, written in the 16th century for the Emperor Akbar (1566-1605), is recognised by some scholars as providing evidence of the origins of Kathak although this term was not applied to dance until later. The manuscript classifies two forms of nṛtta. One

---

[23] Although regional styles are local they are part of the śāstra tradition and are not folk dance forms.

[24] Moghul is a corruption of a Persian word for Mongol, a race of people from Central Asia (Mongolia). Barbur, a descendent of Genghis Khan, led the invasion.

type uses set pieces and is highly structured but the other is flexible and allows more freedom within a broad framework. It appears to describe the regional, desī styles that 'coalesced into a distinct tradition... from which the present day dance styles... are directly derived' (Bose 1991, p.2). Common reference to Kathak being a 500-year-old tradition refers to this although the exact relationship of today's styles to these older desī forms is not fully understood.

The Persian rulers were Muslims and found the religious aspects of Hindu dance unsuitable. The tradition gradually became more secular, absorbing Persian influences from a variety of sources.[25] Thumri (songs) developed using non-religious poetry, the dancer capturing the mood and narrative using natya elements. The emphasis shifted towards nṛtta aspects in general. Some Persian terms entered the vocabulary with the influx of Persian dancers, for example, amad (the entry) the opening of a performance or savaal javaab, for the fast question and answer competition between dancer and musician that is a specialisation of Kathak. Persian art introduced interest in geometrical designs and mathematical patterns. This had an impact on dance and music leading to the appearance of more intricate rhythmic aspects.

The Hindu courts of Rajasthan, particularly at Jaipur, continued although subservient to Muslim rule in the main. Akbar the Great married a Rajput princess bringing Hindu dancers under the Emperor's direct patronage. Muslim and Hindu influences mixed together but there was less financial support for the devadāsī in the Hindu temples. In Hindu-dominated Madras this was not the case: Dāsī Aṭṭam, the classical dance style of the devadāsī continued in south India. In the Moghal north, cultured patrons in the shape of the Emperor and the provincial Rajas and Nawabs encouraged the development of a secular tradition.[26] The dancers did not use great amounts of space. The wealthy audience were in close proximity to them and usually sat on embroidered floor spreads or carpets, leaning against cushions. (Thrones were not used until later in the period). The change in performance context, from temple to palace, also led to new dress codes as the court dancers adopted Persian style costumes. These still provide a model for clothing choices in Kathak today. In the 18th century Kathak had strong links in the eastern region of Uttar Pradesh but developments moved to Lucknow.

The 19th century saw the rise of British power in India and the consolidation of two

---

[25] Some writers believe the Persian influence is overstated.

[26] Rajas and Nawobs were the local princes or rulers of smaller regions under the dominion of the Emperor.

major gharanas (schools) of Kathak at Jaipur and Lucknow.[27] The former emphasised nṛtta elements and technical expertise while the latter focused on expressive qualities.[28] In 1847 Nawob Wajid Ali Shah came to the provincial throne of Oudh. An enthusiastic supporter of the arts, he established a training centre for dancers and gave lavish court entertainments at Lucknow. This was the era for the particular development of Thumri, and Hindu religious stories still persisted, the tradition not having been entirely secularised. The Nawob's dance guru (teacher) was Thakur Prasad who probably originated from the Jaipur area of Rajasthan.

Moghul rule declined economically and politically. In 1856 Oudh was annexed and its court abolished by the British who took full control of India in 1857, although this was not formalised until 1858. Queen Victoria was crowned Empress of India in 1876 in a symbolic gesture of British sovereignty. Prasad and his two nephews, Bindadin Maharaj and Kalka Prasad continued to develop Kathak. Some scholars list them as Prasad's sons but they may descend from his brother Durga (Banerji 1982). One thing is key; the lineage of guru to disciple (teacher to pupil) is very important in Indian dance traditions.

Lineage

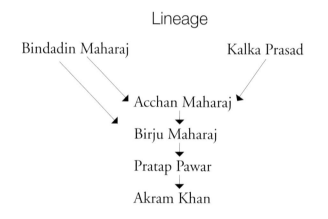

Bindadin was known for his graceful, expressive nṛtya qualities while Kalka specialised in nṛtta, the mastery of rhythm. Thus Lucknow became strong in both aspects of Kathak; 'lyrical grace and technical precision' (Massey 1989, p.80). Kalka Prasad's son, Acchan was Birju Maharaj's father and teacher.[29] Birju (born 1937) was also taught by Bindadin and thus incorporated both styles. He was the guru of Pratap Pawar who in his turn taught

---

[27] Gharana indicates something more than a school, suggesting a household and also a style.

[28] Over time the styles at Jaipur and Lucknow developed variations but more recently, with many dancers now learning both, there has been some reintegration.

[29] Another of Kalka's sons, Lacchu, (died 1978) choreographed films in Bombay.

Akram Khan, thus making Khan a direct descendent of the Lucknow style. Birju Maharaj performing in London, with Pawar and Khan, is described as follows,

> hands pattering like raindrops. Feet drumming the waves of the sea, body hunched comically to show the small-brained struttings of a peacock... his volatile features and amazingly articulate hands throwing up bright seashells of imagery. (Mackrell, 2001, n.p.)

In summary, Kathak 'carries the imprint of both the temple and the court... [it] developed as a chamber art, intended for performance before an intimate gathering' (Khokar 1979, p.97). It is the only classical dance style in India that has links with Muslim culture.

The twentieth century – decline

A period of decline in all the classical dance forms set in around the turn of the 19th century. Scholars do not agree as to the reasons. It is possible that loss of financial support from the courts meant that dancers moved elsewhere and some critics state that brothels hosted performances. The social status of the dancer declined and perhaps modern industrialisation also discouraged the nautch tradition, as the dance was known in some quarters. The decrease of patronage under British colonial rule may have been compounded by the fact that wealthy Indians, educated in Western traditions, were hostile to what seemed a debased Indian tradition. Victorian morality may have led to a misunderstanding of the devadāsī tradition. The dancers may indeed have been prostitutes. Mahatma Gandhi stated that many temples were 'no better than brothels' (Gandhi quoted by Massey in Iyer 1997, p.19).

Revival – a cultural renaissance

Whether the nautch girls used more erotic gestures or whether they kept the tradition alive, as some scholars claim, is difficult to assess. The relationship between the nautch and current classical styles is not fully understood. What is clear is that a cultural renaissance took place after Indian Independence in 1947. The later years of the 20th century saw systematic research of the Sanskrit manuscripts and the temple sculptures. Upper class (Brahmin) Indians began to rebuild and value their national traditions. For example the great Bengali poet, Rabindranath Tagore founded a school in 1901, 'with (later) assistance from the English educator Leonard Elmhirst who had founded Dartington Hall', in which all the arts, including dance, were on the curriculum (Massey in Iyer 1997, p.20).[30] In South India two Brahmins, E. Krishna Iyer and Rukmeni Devi helped rescue the Dasi Attam temple tradition (also known as Sadir) and make it socially acceptable. They gave it a new name, Bharātaataam.

A changing performance milieu – into the theatre

It is not possible to note all the contributors who played a part in developing new theatre-based forms of Indian dance but they include Uday Shankar who built an international reputation as a dancer. The famous Russian ballerina, Anna Pavlova, saw him dancing in a charity show in London in 1924 and invited him to perform with her ballet company. Eventually he embarked on a solo career, creating his own eclectic style that included a grounding in Bharata Natyam and Kathakali plus 'steps from Bengali folk dances, movements from the Oriental dances of Ruth St Denis, ideas from Indian sculpture and painting, and much else' (Hall 1982, p.6).[31] He established his own company and toured extensively (basing himself at Dartington Hall for a time) before opening a school in India in 1938. Similarly innovative was Ram Gopal who toured the USA and made his London début in 1939. Menaka (Lady Lila Sokhey) established a dance company that won prizes at the 1936 International Dance Olympiad at the Olympic Games. Her productions, based on the traditional stories of Vishnu and Krishna, developed the theatrical possibilities of Kathak and used several different classical styles.[32] Themes also changed and now broached 'politics, philosophy of life or current social problems' (Banerji 1982, p.51). In the later 20th century Kathak dancers also appeared in India's nascent film industry and are thus connected to the development of today's eclectic Bollywood style.

The performance context moved away from the spatial restrictions of chamber presentations into more theatrical settings.

The interest is in adapting Kathak ... for the modern stage ... this presents an interesting challenge, for the theatres today contain a larger audience than was ever possible in either

---

[30] See further connections to Dartington Hall in the sections on Michael Hulls and Andy Cowton.

[31] Ruth St Denis – American modern dancer and choreographer, who with Ted Shawn founded the seminal Denishawn School in 1915. Martha Graham was a student there.

[32] These innovators were criticised by some for not being authentic. Experimenting with traditional forms was perhaps seen as a challenge to the orthodox canon that others were struggling to rebuild.

the temple courtyard or the intimate atmosphere of ... the select company of connoisseurs. (Massey 1989, p.81)

Classical styles of Indian dance are now taught and performed in many countries, spreading internationally through post colonial migration. Indian Independence changed the political borders within the subcontinent and a narrow identification with one country no longer reflects the geographic spread. Scholars now refer to these styles as South Asian dance.

Kathak: an introduction to the technique, music and costume

The *Bibliography and Resources* section lists some useful visual resources and websites for this dance style for those unfamiliar with it.

Although Kathak is traditionally a solo form there has been variation over time, the painting of Akbar the Great for example on page 25 depicts him watching a duet. Kathak today retains its courtly qualities of well-mannered formality while emphasising incisive percussive attack, lyrical fluidity and a sense of calm control. It is generally characterised by dexterity, precision, speed, grace, agility and musicality. Kathak is known for its tatkar or footwork, in which the dancer's feet become percussion instruments. Ankle bells (ghungurus) enhance the effect. It is divided into nṛtta (abstract enjoyment of shape, design and rhythm) and nṛtya (expression of emotions, moods and stories). The latter is allusive rather than literally mimetic. It conveys the atmosphere and mood inherent in the story. The plot is given only in outline.

Rasa – aesthetic experience

Kathak is not just an empty display of bravura technique, however exhilarating it is to watch. Rasa (sentiment) and bhāva (mood) are important concepts. Rasa is difficult to translate but might best be understood as the emotional states that give a particular flavour to a work. They produce an 'unexpressible inward experience... [a] sort of supernatural delight' (Banerji 1990, p.205). Thus, elements like stage décor and properties are not included because 'the spectator is fully to exercise his own imagination' (Khokar 1979, p.54). The dancer aims to project feelings and moods through the use of nṛtya elements in order to evoke a deep imaginative response in the spectator. Rasa thus engenders an over-powering aesthetic experience that is equated with ecstatic spiritual states and is part of the religious heritage of the dance. There are nine principle types of rasa, classified into particular emotions.[33] (see Table 1)

Nṛtya conveys these moods and feelings through the dancer's use of abhinaya, typically these are expressive movements performed to carry the meaning of a song or poem, though

---

[33] Eight were originally classified in the Nātyaśāstra and a ninth was added later.

Table

This lists the rasa (Banerji 1990, p.205). Column three gives alternative choices of terms (Massey 1989, p.xvii).

Rasa			Associated deity	Associated Colour
sringara	erotic	love	Vishnu	light green
vira	heroic	heroism	Indra	light orange
raudra	furious	anger	Rudra	red
bibhatsa	disgustful	disgust	Śiva as Mahakala	blue
hasya	comic	humour	Pramatha	white
adbhata	marvellous	wonder	Brahma	yellow
karuna	pathetic	pathos	Yama	ash
bhayanaka	terrible	terror	Kala	black
santa	quietistic	serenity	Narayana	white

their ability to lend beauty is still important.[34] These movements are classified in great detail for example, there are thirty six different glances of the eyes, seven movements of the eyebrows, sixty seven hand gestures (hastas), and thirty two foot movements (caris).

Karanas and the basic building blocks of movement

The basic posture is upright, elegant and well balanced. The head is held high but with an easy neck and relaxed, open shoulders. The legs are straight with heels together and slightly turned out. Kathak does not favour the demi plié or bent-kneed position taken as the basic stance in Bharata Natyam. A characteristic position of the arms during tatkar is to bend the elbows sideways and bring the 'hands [to] chest level ... forearms parallel to the chest, palms facing down and the finger tips of each hand tip to tip (Bhavnani 1979, p.40). Different single actions for example, caris (movements of one leg) and sthanas (postures or shapes) combine to make composite movements called karanas. These are the basic building blocks or units of dance, preserved on the temple walls from ancient times. Each is best thought of as a small nexus of movement rather than as a static position.

[34] In addition to body gestures there are three other techniques of abhinaya: accompaniment; costume and make up; and acting or the ability to create physical manifestations of emotional states.

Kathak does not use the rigid system of hastas (codified hand gestures that carry meaning) found in Bharata Natyam.[35] In Kathak hastas have a dual function; some are used for nṛtta and carry no meaning while others echo the changing nṛttya moods and tell the fundamentals of the stories. Dancers learn some of the conventional hastas but not their names because the whole body is expressive, not only the hands. For example, 'if the dancer intends to represent the moon, not only will his hands show the ... hasta but his body will also bend in an arch to suggest the idea' (Rao, M., in Anonymous 1963, p.45). Kathak does not prescribe the movement in detail but indicates the general type, allowing the dancer to bring individuality and creativity to their choices. This freedom applies to both nṛtta and nṛttya aspects.

Tatkar – footwork

Nṛtta aspects are subdivided into two contrasting qualities or styles, 'tandava represents virility and energy while lasya represents delicacy and grace' (Bose 1991, p.139). These two are seen as complementary masculine and feminine characteristics but are performed by dancers of either gender.[36] Tatkar is a key feature of nṛtta and is what gives Kathak its unique character. Layakari or intricate time-measurement is a key skill because the dancer parallels and counterpoints complex subdivisions of the accompanying rhythm in a percussive and almost mathematical use of the feet against the floor. The aim is to slap the foot rather than stamp and 'what is significant is not the mere striking out of these beats but the control of sound, the variation in loud and soft beats, in clear and open sound... in the gradual release and reining in of energy... [and] in the almost inaudible lifting of a foot during a pause' (Samson 1987, p.85).

Different parts of the feet are used. For example, in kunchita a toe or front part of the foot strikes the ground, or one foot stamps behind the other, in tharr a dancer 'drags the thumb of one foot raising the remaining portion of the foot' (Banerji 1982, p.148). Each movement produces a different sound in the ankle bells and is represented by a bole (a spoken rhythmic syllable). Birju Maharaj's version is given in the quotation below but there are different technical interpretations of the boles which serves to illustrate their complexity.

---

[35] Kathak tends to use the term hasta, mudra is another term in more general use.

[36] The Nātyaśāstra says tandava is used for praise. It is uncertain at what point male and female dancers alike performed this – perhaps from the beginning. The karanas on the temples at a later date depict only female dancers but this may be to do with the devadāsī tradition at this point.

A flat step pushed from back to front (thei); the heel pushed from back to front (tat); heel down (ki, gi, etc); striking with the outer portion of the foot (ghi); toes striking the ground behind (na). (Kippen, 1996, n.p)

Footwork is beaten directly beneath the body so the torso stays balanced elegantly over the support. There is no bounce in the knees as might occur in tap dancing, though the knees stay slightly relaxed. The torso is not rigid and 'the movements of the upper part of the body... [can] capture... by just suggesting, the sound-effects of the boles' (Saxena, S., in Anonymous 1963, p.51). Footwork is taken at three speeds, slow, medium and fast (further described in the section on music). Greater speed should not result in scanty movement or a rushed appearance. Any accompanying arm movements are graceful but can emphasise defined lines and sometimes have a firm, almost photographic clarity. Dancers learn the complexities of the tal (rhythms) by reciting the boles aloud, listening to their bells, and marking the rhythm (kriya) by clapping it or counting silently on their fingers tips.

Chakkar or spins

Phrases of footwork often involve chakkar (pivot turns), which although they are performed at great speed must be controlled. The dancer spins on the heel or back part of the foot and remains on the spot, with no distortion of bodyline, abbreviation, or jerkiness in the arm movements. Multiple turns are timed to complete fast phrases of footwork so that the dancer arrives at the sum with a flourish. The sum is a moment of climax and is the first beat of the new phrase of music. The dancer must arrive simultaneously with it and remain still and poised. This is not always easy since they and the musicians sometimes improvise.

The structure and format of a classical Kathak performance

A traditional solo performance contains a variety of nṛtta and nṛtya elements and consists of a series of separate, short items that build to a climax. Kathak sets out a framework for this but does not usually follow set compositions. The dancer brings personal choice to bear.

Salutation

The first dance item is usually a salutation to the stage.[37]

---

[37] Known as the Salaam – the Persian word for salutation.

Hands are cupped together above the head and the fingers open out like a flower... (pushpanjali hasta), as the hands come down towards the chest. They are then tilted forwards as if offering flowers to the stage. There then follows the water offering and obeisance to the presiding deity... [it] ends with a namashka... the Hindu salutation... [or] a Muslim salaami... [in which] the right hand alone is used... the fingers are held together and very slightly bent. The thumb rests across the palm. The hand is then raised to touch the forehead while the head is bowed as a mark of respect. (Massey 1989, pp.96-97)

Amad and Thaat – a slow introduction to the performance

The amad or entry is slow and uses one of the typical poses. Thaat then follows. It is decorative and graceful. Though variations are possible, typically the dancer stands

erect, relaxed, looking straight ahead ... with the left hand raised a little over and to the side of the head, right hand extended to the right, in line with the shoulder ... as if absorbing the floating waves of the music ...[he] begins to sway lightly, while moving his hands very gently at the wrists. He also embellishes with a slight, gliding side-ways movement of the neck. (Khokar 1988, p.47)

Isolations, for example, the movement of the neck described above, are called rechakas.

Gaths – nṛtya elements

Gaths (storytelling episodes) introduce nṛtya for the first time. Both codified and expressive gestures are used. The dancer may take several themes and the items do not need to be connected or in any particular order. Gath nikas sketch the ideas that are then developed in the ghat bhāva. Chaals or gatis (walks) and the chosen movements give clues as to any character in the story or suggest animals, as for example the peacock gait. It is not represen-tational mime. It does not mimic the animal or character but instead brings out the essential qualities or emotional states. Typically characters are signified, or alluded to, rather than being fully enacted for an audience well versed in the stories.

Krishna... is shown by the hands in the attitude of holding his flute, or by the appropriate gesture for the peacock feathers he wears in his head-dress. Śiva is characterised by the snake around his neck or the crescent moon on his head, Rādhā by drawing the veil... over her face. (Massey 1989, p.98).

A popular story is that of Rādhā going to fetch water from the well. She is returning with a full pitcher when a playful Krishna throws a stone and breaks it. Rādhā is soaked and although she is secretly pleased to encounter him she pretends to be angry. She brushes Krishna aside and walks away trying to dry her skirt as she goes. The dancer, as always, plays all the roles and interplay is subtle, the mischievous quality of the God alternating with the woman's mock anger. Each change of character is assisted by the use of a palta (an abstract gesture or turning action) to separate the parts, for example the dancer turns to face the opposite side for each.

Tukras and Torahs – the performance speeds to a climax with nṛtta and tatkar

Pure dance tukras usually follow and the performance begins to speed up through these next items. A tukra is a short phrase of tatkar lasting six or seven bars of the basic timescale at the end of which the dancer takes a typical Kathak position and holds it for one bar, for example, arms swept aloft with palms outwards. The dancer reproduces the sounds of the accompaniment in the ankle bells and movement becomes more vigorous (tandav). Torah are similar to tukra. The dancer recites the boles aloud for the audience to hear, setting out increasingly elaborate cycles of beats that are then made visible by the dancer's movement. Torah makes use of the body,

> the hands dash forward, return and do a variety of movements mostly about the level of the chest ... the highlight ... is the spin ... towards the close of the composition, the dancer undertakes a body-spin, three times or in multiples of three ensuring that the last beat of the display coincides with [the sum]. (Khokar 1988, p.48)

When a Torha is repeated three times in succession it becomes a tohai. In the Jaipur school the speed was doubled with each repetition. A Kavita Torah is performed to the recitation of a poem. Phrases now gradually become longer and more complex as the dancer and musicians warm up. The dancer may match or counterpoint the accompanying rhythms. Parmelus and parans are the fastest items and often bring the performance to its climax,

> complicated combinations and permutations in fractional beats that criss-cross and divide the main beats, often going against the mainstream of the actual beats and ending once again with the tihai or thrice-repeated conclusion that falls incredibly and calculatedly on the sum. (Samson 1987, p.85).

Fast items may take the form of an unrehearsed, improvised competition, the dancer and musicians challenging each other to greater complexity, in a question and answer format called a savaal javaab or jugal bandi. This is a thrilling and well-known aspect of Kathak.

Music

South Asian music is based on melody and rhythm rather than harmony (the base for European forms). From medieval times, music and dance in Kathak have developed a special relationship, becoming interdependent allied arts. Typically accompaniment is provided by two musicians, one often uses a stringed instrument (such as the stangi) played with a bow to give melody and the other, a percussionist, creates rhythm using a long, double-ended drum (pakhawaj) plus a pair of smaller upright drums (named tabla, after the right hand one of these) all of which are beaten by hand. Traditionally the pakhawaj accompanies tatkar sections of dance and any melody ceases. Thumri (songs) have existed for some time as a musical form.[38] Bindadin Maharaj (1830-1918) wrote many more of these and also dadra and ghazal, which are other types of poetry, set to music. Thus there may also be a singer who accompanies some of the slower items. In the past the dancer may sometimes have sung these. The ankle bells echo the words in the same way as they reproduce and make visible the musical rhythms. There are some poems where the dancer repeatedly sings a line and then interprets it in different ways using nritya aspects, mainly the face and eyes.

Each piece of music is in one particular mood and interest is in the time variations (fast, medium, slow). The mood changes when one musical item follows another. The Persian influence can be felt in the geometrical and mathematical precision of the complex tal (rhythmical patterns). Time measurement is determined by laya, which is a key concept. It determines the speed or rhythm, hence layakari, the dancer's mastery of the variations of this. A musical phrase usually repeats within a given time scale and 'provides the dancer and percussionist with an ever-present and constant time measure' of which there are many, but trital is perhaps the most popular (Massey 1989, p.84). The percussionist sets the rhythm and plays, for example a measure of 16, 12 or 6 beats. The table below is adapted from Massey (1989, p.85). It illustrates the first set of beats within a trital. Beats are not counted by number but by using rhythmic syllables or boles, the musician and the dancer each having their own system.[39] It can be seen that two tabla beats are counted for each dance

---

[38] Nawob Wajid Ali Shah wrote many in the 19th century.

[39] Some dance boles are referred to as the Natwari boles because of the belief that when Krishna (Natwari) was a boy the ball he was playing with fell into the river. When he went to retrieve it he was bitten on the leg by the multi-headed serpent Kaliya. He proceeded to fight and subdue this monster and then performed a victory dance on its hoods which produced the sounds of tha, thei and tat.

beat. Three tabla beats are stressed in the whole measure, on counts 1, 5, and 13 and this corresponds to 1, 3, and 7 for the dance. Three accents are stressed, making it a trital, but because beat 9 is khali, or empty of stress, this gives an asymmetrical feel to the ongoing pulse. Dancers learn these complex patterns by reciting the boles and clapping them. In the case of the trital below the empty beat, 5, is not clapped.

Tabla Boles	Dha	dhin	dhin	dha	Dha	dhin	dhin	dha	Dha	thin	thin	tha	Tha	dhin	dhin	dhat
	1	2	3	4	**5**	6	7	8	(9)	10	11	12	**13**	14	15	16
Dance Boles	tha – a		thei – ee		thé – ee		tha – th		aa – a		thé – ee		thé – ee		tha – th	
	1		2		**3**		4		(5)		6		**7**		8	

Three speeds increase incrementally in respect of the pace set by the slow version which is called tha. Doon doubles this to a medium speed and is twice that of tha, chaugun (fast) doubles this again and is four times the speed of tha. There is also eight times the speed (athgun) although this is rare. For example, a slow two-count clap would double to a medium speed with 4 claps and then to 8 fast claps and finally 16 rapid ones. There are also complex patterns involving fractions of tha, for example one and half times the speed. The musician and dancer share great rhythmical dexterity as a key skill. When there is improvised interplay (savaal javaab) between music and dance the

> dancer must know within a beat what the drummer is going to play ... some sequences extend over a hundred boles ... the task of the dancer becomes exceedingly difficult. Nevertheless, the essential rapport between dancer and drummer must be maintained ... the pleasure lies in the pure aesthetic enjoyment of the rhythm. (Massey 1989, pp.99-100).

Costume

Kathak costume has changed over time. Colour choices were often linked to the significant rasa to be evoked (see Table p.33). The 16th century painting of Akbar the Great provides evidence of unusual costumes at that point. The dancers wear clothes that in their shortness are different to those the courtiers are wearing.

Men wore a jacket and the women a choli, a fitted blouse with short sleeves which leaves the midriff bare. Both had tight trousers called a 'chust pajama'. Over these they wore plissé skirts made of stiff material in three tiers the longest of which reached several inches above the knee ... they also wore, over their shoulders, a transparent scarf of silk or muslin, known as an 'orhni'... the headdress normally consisted of a muslin turban, though the character of Krishna was identified with a mukut or crown. (Massey 1989, p.76)

Later, dancers adopted the style of dress favoured during the reign of Akbar's son. This style did not remain fashionable for long at court but continued to be popular with dancers. Numerous Rajastani miniatures from the 17th and 18th centuries show dancers in this type of costume. Women wore a brightly coloured 'chust pajama' and a transparent dress (an angarkha).

The soft, flowing, bell-shaped skirt was of full length and, like the sleeves, was left unlined. For women, an embroidered waistcoat of rich satin emphasised the body line. Men wore a double-breasted 'angarkha' which fastened on the left, with their 'chust pajama'. The women also wore gossamer 'orhni'. The palms of their hands and bare feet were dyed with henna ... the full skirt fanned out at every fast movement, accentuating the fluidity of the dance, and yet transparent enough to reveal the outline of the figure and perfection of the pose when the dancer was still. (Massey 1989, p.77)

A variety of styles are permitted today. The classical dancer can make individual choices from costumes that are both Hindu and Muslim in origin. The former uses a long, full skirt (ghaagra), gathered tightly at the waist and decorated by a gold or silver border.

Narrow silver or gold bands radiate all the way from waist to hem... the choli... is usually of a contrasting colour and has embroidered sleeve-bands. The light, transparent orhni is interwoven with gold patterns and draped over the head and left shoulder... bracelets, armlets and necklaces are of gold... heavy earrings... are set with precious or semi-precious stones. Their weight is taken off the earlobes by fine gold chains or... ropes of tiny seed-pearls which hook into the hair. A jewelled 'tika' is suspended in the middle of the forehead.[40] (Massey 1989, p.82)

Another variation for women involves adapting a sari for dancing (normally worn over the left shoulder) by wrapping it around the waist and leaving the long end to hang down on the left side. Similarly men can wear: a large silk loincloth (dhoti), draped around the waist and through the legs, to create a loose trouser-like effect; a silk scarf tied around the waist; the

---

[40] Tika – like a brooch that lies flat against the forehead.

A pair of girls with joined hands performing a Kathal Dance, Mughal Aurangzeb, period c.1675. Victoria and Albert Museum, London.

Prince with a falcon.

upper torso bare except for a sacred thread; and sometimes a loose fitting, short sleeved jacket. Both men and women wear elaborate jewellery.

Muslim versions are perhaps the most favoured by dancers of today and are therefore the more familiar of the possible choices to audiences. The hem of the anghakha is shortened typically to calf length and fewer jewels are worn although it is not unusual for women to wear earrings, pearl necklaces, armbands and bracelets. A fan-shaped piece of jewellery sometimes lies flat to the head and, of course, brass ankle bells (ghungurus) are worn. Men often wear a traditional panjabi kurtha (tunic or angarkha).

South Asian and Contemporary Dance in the UK

Exotic display

The 19th century in Europe saw a fashion for oriental themes in both Romantic and Classical Ballet. Although exoticism was the main interest, costumes and plots appear to have demonstrated some knowledge of the tradition that the ballets were drawing on. For example, Filippo Taglioni's *Le Dieu et la Bayadère* (1830) for his ballerina daughter used the devadesi as a starting point and included a character in the role of the Hindu God, Brahma. Interest in temple dancers continued: Jean Coralli's *La Péri* (1843) with Carlotta Grisi in the tile role; and Marius Petipa's *La Bayadère* (1877).[41] Two lithographs reproduced in Beaumont (1949) show Grisi sporting a short choli with bare midriff and Marie Taglioni wearing a long floating stole, pearl necklaces, arm bands, bracelets, forehead decoration, a skirt with three tiers/hems, and a loose strip of fabric over the left shoulder and hanging from the waist. The references to traditional Kathak costumes are clear. Current versions of Petipa's *La Bayadère* use classical ballet tutus but hint at the orhni with a short strip of fabric trailing from the dancers' arms.

Interest in the exotic continued in the early 20th century, for example, Michel Fokine's *Le Dieu Bleu* (1912) with Vaslav Nijinsky in the role of Krishna. Fokine, a choreographer in the vanguard of modern ballet, experimented with new sources of vocabulary. He 'wished to use the angular poses of the limbs, the childishly-bent head, the turned-up palms and curved fingers characteristic of Hindu sculpture' (Beaumont 1945, pp.86-87). The significance of certain symbols in South Asian dance seems to have been understood since Nijinsky stepped out from a giant lotus flower holding 'a reed pipe' in his hand (Beaumont 1945, p.98).[42]

Pavlova's interest in Uday Shankar has been noted earlier. His touring helped to create interest in South Asian dance forms. He also trained European dancers to perform with his

---

[41] Marie Taglioni and Carlotta Grisi were two of the greatest ballerinas of the Romantic era in ballet. Grisi was the first Giselle.

[42] It is traditional for Krishna to be depicted playing a pipe. There is a hasta specifically illustrating the lotus flower. The lotus is symbolic of the desire of the soul for heaven or Nirvana; its roots grow deep in the mud, the bud grows up through the water and then flowers in the sun.

Marie Taglioni in *La Bayadère*, from the lithograph by A.E. Chalon.

Carlotta Grisi in *La Péri*, from a lithograph by J. Brandard.

company including Simkie (the French Simone Barbière) who was his own dance partner. Ram Gopal shared Shankar's eclectic approach to performance. He studied many different dance forms including Kathakali, Bharata Natyam and Ballet and like Shankar was criticised in his latter years for this approach. In 1939 however he made his London début dancing to full houses and 'was invited to tea with Queen Mary' (Anonymous 2003b, p.31). He made London his home in 1947 and appeared in an acting role in the film, *Elephant Walk* (1951) in which he also choreographed a dance sequence. In 1962 he opened his Academy for Indian Dance and Music in London. The Asian Music Circle eventually established the first long lasting series of dance classes in 1966 when Krishna Rao and his wife were brought over to deliver regular Bharata Natyam classes. There was a limited choice of styles at this point but this was to change.

Establishing a UK performance base

In the 1970s there was a large-scale migration of Asian families to the UK, particularly from Uganda when the dictator Idi Amin expelled all Asians. This led to increasing audiences and more visiting artists although performances were usually within smaller, non-theatrical venues. These were a way of keeping ties with the homeland but also became a way of developing new cultural traditions in the UK. The opening of the Bhavan Institute in 1972 gave a further impetus and provided lessons although students still needed to travel to India to hone their performance skills. During the early 1970s even Contemporary Dance struggled to build an identity and gain support within a cultural environment where Ballet was the dominant style. American-influenced forms of Contemporary Dance introduced into the UK in the late 1960s were gradually evolving into British styles with the emergence of choreographers such as Richard Alston, Siobhan Davies, Robert North, Rosemary Butcher and Christopher Bruce. There are two excellent sources of information in respect of these developments so this will not be repeated here. (See Jordan (1992) and Mackrell (1992).) South Asian styles were thus competing for attention against this background.

In 1979 Tara Rajkumar, a Mohini dancer, founded the Academy of Indian Dance (now known as the Akademi) to build audiences and raise awareness. It became pivotal in encouraging more systematic support from the Arts Council. A seminar in 1982 investigated issues raised by Naseem Khan's 1976 report, *The Arts that Britain Ignores*. This had recommended the planning of 'strategic policies aimed at establishing a better environment and targeted funding for minority arts' (Bannerman, 2004, p.2). The seminar was also attended by dance luminaries from the Ballet and Contemporary worlds and Massey pointed out that a range of backgrounds for performers (Asian-born, UK-born Asians, and European artists) meant that South Asian forms should no longer be seen as minority ethnic styles (Kansara 1982). This forced a reconsideration of the policies that supported South Asian arts and led to significant developments in the 1980s.

Triveni Dance Company founded by Priya and Pratap Pawar in 1980, among others, toured extensively. In 1983 the Academy commissioned a dance drama based on Kipling's story of Mowgli. The use of a non-religious theme and mix of classical styles was a bold step and showed that a new sensibility could be developed in the UK context. *The Adventures of Mowgli*, with Pratap Pawar as Shere Khan and the young Akram Khan, toured to mainstream stages. It brought in new audiences but also initiated a debate about the impact of European theatrical traditions upon classical dance. Views were split; some favoured the protection of the heritage and others felt that new considerations should be brought to bear. To some extent these opposing tensions still obtain. See Sanders (2004c) for a discussion of the work of Shobana Jeyasingh who evolved her own contemporary voice within Bharata Natyam. The dance scene proliferated; Alpana Sengupta, Nilima Devi, Nahid Saddiqui, Sonia Sabri are all well known Kathak exponents. It produced performers who work in a traditional manner in a wide variety of different classical styles and also those performers seeking to reflect a UK identity.

Coming of Age

A momentum was established that became sympathetic to innovation and encouraged a range of approaches, including the use of composers from Western traditions. The work of Shobana Jeyasingh within Bharata Natyam has already been mentioned and Akram Khan is not alone in making work that confounds traditional distinctions between styles. Mavin Khoo, trained in Bharata Natyam and Classical Ballet, explores the links between these two. 'The heritage versus contemporary divide has become sufficiently permeable that they [Khan and Khoo] ... perform traditional concerts as well as creating contemporary dance works' (Bannerman, 2004, p.2). The wide variety of South Asian forms now on offer in the UK can be explored in the CD-ROM listed in the *Bibliography and Resources* section. There are many performers who are UK trained and there are several regional organisations supporting South Asian dance, for example, Kadam in Bedford.

The growing confidence is shown by the large scale projects organised by the Akademi at prestigious venues: the *Coming of Age* event at the South Bank Centre, London, 2001; the symposium, *Unwrapped*, at the Royal Opera House 2002 which explored South Asian aesthetics and the developing UK identity (Ramphal 2002); and *Escapade* in 2003, also at the South Bank Centre, a large-scale, outdoor, mixed media event. Contemporary work shows the inclusion of a variety of styles, for example, martial arts, and there is also growing popular interest in Bollywood and club culture styles. Agencies such as Sampad provide opportunities for showcasing youth dance. They also commission artists, such as Sonia Sabri's *drishti* (2001) a dialogue between Kathak, music and digital design. South Asian Dance forms are offered at various levels within the education system. The Imperial Society of Teachers of Dancing, a provider of vocational dance examinations in the UK, offers children's grades in Bharata Natyam and Kathak; some Higher Education institutions include modules of South Asian dance within their degree courses; and London Contemporary Dance School launched a BA (Honours) in Contemporary Dance, with South Asian dance as a specialism in September 2004. Kadam also publishes a specialist journal, *Pulse*.

There have been some examples of choreographers working across the traditional boundaries although this is still relatively rare; Richard Alston's *Delicious Arbor* (1993) for Shobana Jeyasingh's company and Nahid Saddiqui's *Krishna* (2003) for the Birmingham Royal Ballet. As Iyer sums up:

> there has been a surge in dance activity aimed at expanding and merging forms, rejecting traditional content and seeking to be more attuned to contemporary life while articulating the specificity of ... working in Britain. And yet, in the background, there is also a call to adhere to traditional values, to preserve the authenticity of the traditions... the resulting landscape is composite. (Iyer 1997, p.3)

Bibliography and Resources for South Asian Dance

Anonymous. *Classical and Folk Dances of India*, Bombay: Marg Publications. 1963

Anonymous. Obituaries, Ram Gopal. *The Times*, p.31. October 14th, 2003

Banerji, P. *Kathak Through the Ages*, New Delhi: Cosmo Publications. 1982

Banerji, S. S. *A Companion to Indian Music and Dance*, Delhi: Sri Satguru Publications. 1990

Bannerman, C. *South Asian Diaspora Dance in Britain*. SALIDAA (South Asian Diaspora Literature and Arts Archive), www.salida.org.uk, accessed 08/01/04.

Bhavnani, E. *The Dance in India*, Bombay: Taraporevala's Treasure House of Books. 1979

Bose, M. *Movement and Mimesis: the idea of dance in the Sanskritic Tradition*, Dordrecht/Boston/London: Kluwer Academic. 1991

Coomaraswamy, A., K. *The Dance of Shiva*, New York:Dover. 1985

Hall, F., in B. Kansara (ed), *Academy of Indian Dance Seminar: the contribution of Indian Dance to British Culture*, Commonwealth Institute.1982,

Iyer, A., (ed), *South Asian Dance: the British Experience*, Harwood Academic, Choreography and Dance: an International Journal. 1997

Kansara, B. (ed), *Academy of Indian Dance Seminar. The contribution of Indian Dance to British Culture*, Commonwealth Institute. 1982

Khokar, M. *Traditions of Indian Classical Dance*, London: Peter Owen. 1979

Khokar, M. *The Splendours of Indian Dance*, New Delhi: Himalayan Books. 1988

Kippen, J., and Bel, A. 'Lucknow Kathak Dance.' article reprinted from *Bansuri*, Volume 13, 1996, www.pathcom.com/~ericp/kathak. accessed 08/01/04

Mackrell, J. 'Legacy of Tradition.' *The Guardian*, n.p. July 12, 2001

Massey, R. a. J. *Dances of India: a General Survey and Dancer's Guide*, London: Tricolour Books. 1989

Ramphal, V. 'Roots/Routes.' *Dance Theatre Journal*, 18, 2, 2002. 16-19

Samson, L. *Rhythm in Joy: Classical Indian Dance Traditions*, India: Lustre Press. 1987

Sanders, L. *Choreographer Fact Card: Shobana Jeyasingh*. Natinal Resource Centre for Dance, 2004

Websites for key organisations supporting South Asian Arts

www.akademi.co.uk (offers education workshops)
www.kadam.org.uk
www.sampad.org.uk
www.salidaa.org.uk
www.southasiandance.co.uk
www.theplace.org.uk

Key Visual Resources

Video:

Siksha Kathak: a teacher's resource, which illustrates Kathak technique, available at www.istd.org.uk/southasian or email sales@istd.org.

Spring ReLoaded, www.videoplace.org.uk or email videoplace@theplace.org.uk, includes work by Angika, Shobana Jeyasingh, and Nahid Saddiqui. Akram Khan's *Fix* is on Spring ReLoaded 6 and includes an interview with Khan.

Available from the National Resource Centre for Dance, www.surry.ac.uk/NRCD: *Aranya Amrita* (dance drama of the Dancers Guild of Calcutta):

Making of Maps (1992) Shobana Jeyasingh

Romance... with Footnotes (1993) Shobana Jeyasingh

Return of Spring (1986) Dhananjayan

Rains through Rhythm, GCE A level dance set solo in July 2002 choreographed by Pratap Pawar.

Rush (2003), sponsored by Arts Council England, Dance Books.

CD-ROM:

Living Tradition (2000), produced by Kadam, uses still and moving images and gives a history of South Asian dance in the UK available from www.mantralingua.com.

Dance Current Awareness Bulletin, (DCAB) produced by National Resource Centre for Dance, database of articles published by main dance journals, includes articles on South Asian dance and choreographers, available from www.surry.ac.uk/NRCD.

Part 3

Starting Points for *Rush*

The contributions of the elements.
- *Choreography*
- *Music*
- *Lighting design*

The Choreography

It grew out of interest in the contrast between speed and stillness that Khan had been experimenting with in *Fix*. When dancing at speed he felt an adrenaline response from the audience. He wanted to explore this phenomenon so took the idea of parachute jumpers (the term paragliders mistakenly got into the advertising leaflets and he had to keep it). 'I wanted to research on paragliders who jump off a plane and a few seconds later release their parachute. Those few seconds are known as freefall. I wanted to ... find out what happens to the five senses; smell, touch, taste, hearing, vision during freefall' (Khan 2000a, n.p).

Khan approached the choreography using improvisation that focussed on visualising movements/positions that would directly relate to freefall and the effect on the five senses, posing himself a series of questions; 'what happens to them when adrenaline is high? Is the sense awake or asleep? Is it conscious or not? Is it awake but you are not conscious of it?' Indeed he even undertook a parachute jump in order to investigate the authentic experience and his dancers watched video material of sky divers freefalling. He discovered that immediately after jumping out of the plane 'there is a feeling of complete emptiness, everything is silent and you are blinded by the wind and light, it is disorientating until shock and the senses kick in and everything suddenly becomes very clear' (Khan 2004). This blinding effect is referred to in the original lighting, created by Ann Joseph, when three floor level lamps, visible at the front of the stage, throw out a strong, bright light that bursts onto the dancers at several moments during part one of *Rush*. Michael Hulls refers to these as the moments that Khan wanted to keep when Hulls relit the piece after the première.

Another question arising during the research period was whether spectators and jumpers enjoy a similar and equal adrenaline rush. This led him to another issue:

> if boundaries are taken apart or even erased, so that there are no divisions between the space that the audience are in and the space of the dancers ... (stage), who would become the watcher and who would be the doer? This question ... provoked me to ask the dancers to stand (with their backs to the audience) right on the edge of the stage as the beginning of *Rush*. The dancers became not only the 'doers' but also the spectators. (Khan 2000a, n.p.)

Rush falls into two parts. Khan explains that in addition to the feeling of extreme speed when you jump, you do not know 'what pathway the wind will take you on through the air,

Rehearsal of *Rush* as a work in progress, Brussels. Akram Khan Company.

thus although you know your finishing point you cannot predict exactly how you will get there so there is a sense of spatial freedom' (Khan 2004). In order to capture the experience of being on edge or the fear felt before a parachute jump Khan decided to use a rare Indian time cycle of nine and a half beats for the movement in the first part. It created an uneven pulse that made the dancers anxious since the accompaniment provides no external beat to keep them together. They practised by counting out loud, moved away and then returned to see if they were still in time. In performance they were assisted by calling out the boles (rhythmical syllables used in Kathak) to initiate some of the movement patterns but they still had to rely on each other and hold their own pulse. Khan admits that sometimes this was difficult to achieve, but not being able to guarantee the outcome gave the dancers an alert quality that hinted at the emotion felt during a parachute jump.

They improvised with falling. Khan called out a series of different body parts that had to become heavy to lead the action, such as the head, arms, knees. Then he speeded up the changes with the rule that the dancers continued improvising until they could use the part that he had called out. This produced accidental transitional moments and he tended to keep these as they began to structure the movement. The first part of the dance was experienced as relentless speed by the dancers. Khan explains that in Kathak there is an explosion of energy from the centre of the body which then dissipates but contemporary dance has a different response. The fastest pace is usually judged to be so at that moment when the dancer can no longer control the technique and the movement begins to feel clumsy. Khan challenged his dancers to go beyond 'that imagined fast, moving into that messy domain, getting used to it and finally moving to the point at which you can perceive speed differently' (Khan 2004). He was also interested in where energy travels from and the pathway that it might take; it may explode from the centre but be contained in the hand rather than being released. There were moments of stillness too.

> I have discovered that most paragliders expressed the opinion that when they were in the air 'gliding' – time seemed to stop. It is as if the sound, the feeling of pressure or 'air' against you, the sense of void and the aspect of 'time', all come to standstill … which gives the illusion that time does not exist. (Khan undated)

Khan recalls that after freefall he could remember only certain moments, but with great clarity. This experience was used to create the floor material later in part one where he kneels upstage left and watches the other two dancers. The aim was to create a hovering quality even though the body is on the ground. They worked with the idea of looking through a camera lens when the shutter is clicking rapidly. This produced a sharp, strobe-like effect with different joints suddenly flexing and coming into clear focus.

When jumping out of a plane height, time and distance need to be calculated carefully and this contrasts with the spatial freedom of the unpredictable journey of freefalling, although small changes in body shape can control the pathway to a certain extent. The second part of *Rush* was performed to the pulse of the music and reflected this extreme precision. Khan used different choreographic processes: a section that used walking and nudging movements was structured using chance; random telephone numbers provided the framework whereas other sections were designed with Khan standing outside and directing the visual appearance.

Fix also provided movement material that Khan continued to explore in *Rush*. This includes: a sudden dropping of the weight to sit on the heels and rebounding up; a full plié with elbows flexing sideways in a complementary manner; the right shoulder pushing forward to initiate a carrying forward of the whole arm as the torso leans forward; elbows flexing overhead to bring the hands tapping down behind onto the upper shoulders; a stepping sideways with hand reaching out and in, quickly rotating as it does so; rolling across the floor ending upright with upper torso circling around clockwise and hands drawing to right side, index finger pressed to thumb as if plucking at the air; a straight legged, vertical elevation with both arms reaching forward one above the other, elbows flexing suddenly; and traditional Kathak material such as spinning (chakkars).

Khan designed the costumes, simple black tops and loose fitting trousers based upon the traditional panjabi kurtha (tunics) and pyjamas. There is little embellishment, in keeping with the abstract treatment of the movement material and the strong use made of unison. The material is light and flows slightly with the movement. The use of straps across the back of Moya Michael's tunic draws attention to her femininity. This small change provides a variation on the theme although essentially the costumes are unisex. All Khan's costumes have been simple black or white up to this point in his career.

The Music

Cowton noticed Khan's use of suspension, unison and some key gestures; 'like falling through the air' with arms horizontal and open, or flung backwards in a V shape. He and Khan also talked about the theme from which he was able to form an impression of the type of sounds to look for. He created the accompaniment for *Rush* in two sections. The first is atmospheric and non pulse-based. 'It is more a sound design than musical composition'. Again metal was a favourite choice. Scrap metal and a large thunder sheet[43] produce sounds that are recorded at a slow speed. The idea is to 'create a sound landscape for the dance to inhabit that also suggests a psychological mood not just a physical space. It hints at a musical space or a rhythmic space at certain points'. The collage of sounds is structured in sympathy with Khan's theme. The first section is 'a kind of suspension in space and time, as you might feel when you're falling. The sound is raw and naïve and there is no melody or rhythm to hold onto. Then it starts to develop, sounding more musical with raw elements becoming more organised and recognisable whilst introducing some loud and slightly uncomfortable noise to create a visceral impact. You do not listen purely with a musical ear. You feel it both emotionally and physically (literally) although this reverberative effect is hard to appreciate from the video recording because it is not as loud as in live performances'. One critic

---

[43] A sheet of metal which produces a noise that sounds like thunder when it is shaken.

describes how 'the music begins like swishing water sprinklers then splits the ears' (Ferguson 2000).

Section two is a contrast to section one because 'rhythm is a starting point'. Cowton synchronised his sound tape with a video of Khan's movement, and because he was working with a particular tempo he set his metronome to it, keeping this later because he liked the effect. Apart from the click of the metronome the source of all the remaining sound is metal. This also includes the bell-like sounds. 'Section two is mechanical, cold, didactic, and cerebral in mood.' Cowton created a rhythmical structure which complements, but does not mirror, Khan's percussive language. Cowton uses musical relationships that are polyrhythmic but he does not share the Indian time cycle of nine and half beats Khan used for his dance material. 'You can break down a steady pulse in different ways to create rhythms that sound like it's swinging, or it's methodical or syncopated even though the pulse remains the same'.[44]

He chose to subdivide the pulse into divisions of 6 versus 5 for the different layers of sound. For example, if one strand of sound is counted in six and another is counted in 5 they will share a major accent on the first beat of the bar in bar one and will not coalesce again until bar 6, as illustrated below.

1 2 3 4 5 6 1 2 3 4 5 6 1 2 3 4 5 6 1 2 3 4 5 6 1 2 3 4 5 6 **1** 2 3 4 5 6

1 2 3 4 5 1 2 3 4 5 1 2 3 4 5 1 2 3 4 5 1 2 3 4 5 1 2 3 4 5 **1** 2 3 4 5

Secondary accents will of course also shift their stress although a continuous pulse will remain in evidence. 'It becomes more organic and evolves an elemental quality as sounds become mixed in and rhythms overlap'. Cowton believes in an 'additive synthesis' of effect. This identifies both the manner in which he layers sound together and how the dance and music fit alongside each other. He states that the accompaniment is in 'dialogue with the aesthetic of others, breathing life into each other, but not being a descriptive process or relationship'. The dance and music share a complex rhythmic dexterity but thus have their own identity, neither describes or mimics the other.

[44] Syncopation is when an accent or rhythmical highlight occurs on a normally unaccented part of the bar. This is noticeable in jazz music for example, where the second beat in the bar may be stressed instead of the first.

The Lighting Design

A quotation from Tipton in respect of the significance of the lighting designer reveals the problem Hulls faced by inheriting Ann Joseph's ideas; 'the lighting designer is the super-audience, because it's through the eyes of the lighting designer that the real audience will be seeing the piece' (De Marigny 1993/94, p.12). In some respects therefore a particular interpretation through another pair of eyes now pre-existed as a further constraint on what he might create. Two moments in particular were retained; a sudden, bright flash of light near the beginning and another near the end of part one of the piece.

As with *Fix*, Hulls uses light to create psychological and structural effects. This can be seen in the opening where the dancers enter, walking down stage where they stand waiting facing the empty stage, silhouetted in dim lighting but with their shadows cast strongly behind them. All focus is on the empty area. As the accompaniment gets louder there is a slow fade in light intensity drawing attention to the change in musical structure. In the blackout the now invisible dancers move into the stage area. This creates an atmosphere of tension and expectation.

Fix and *Rush* were to tour together so there were also practical issues to take into account. *Fix* already uses sixteen, high quality profile lights with shutters to make sharp edges of light. These have to be hired and this is expensive. The company would be touring to small-scale venues so there would be problems of time constraints and limited facilities. *Rush* uses softer edged light and is thus also cheaper to produce. Khan's fledgling company had little infrastructure at that time to support it so Hulls felt that the lighting needed to be error proof; special effects like he might create for Maliphant were kept to a minimum. The horizontal, slightly curved edged pathways of soft light that occur shortly after the opening of the piece are created by a series of overlapping ovals using simple parcans (lamps). Soft ovals of light are again visible in the second section of *Rush* where they appear in a fleur-de-lis pattern centre stage and then in horizontal rows, as illustrated below, with four ovals down stage and three upstage into which the trio of dancers slowly back.

Blue is again a favourite colour and appears in a variety of different tonal qualities, although there are not as many lighting states to achieve this effect as might first appear; 'blue and a whiter blue. Perception depends on what colour you have just seen and is affected by this' so the eye sees more shades than are actually used. The stage is bare. A non-specific territory is constructed with no sense of three-dimensional space enclosing it; the white or blue-soaked floor floats within a sea of darkness, the cyclorama and sides of the stage are invisible.

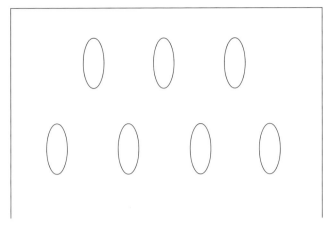

Audience

Rehearsal of *Rush* as a work in progress, Brussels. Akram Khan Company.

Part 4
Using *Rush* in teaching and learning

Ideas and tools for studying Rush.

• *Analysis Summary: starting points, sources for vocabulary, style.*

• *Structural Overview Chart: a broad outline of* Rush.

• *Analysing* Rush*: ideas for practical and theoretical tasks*

• *Making an Analysis: questions to guide the process.*

Analysis Summary

Starting Points

- Varieties of adrenaline rush – performer/spectator interface in live performance participant/spectator in the extreme sport of freefall.
- Energy flow explored in *Fix* (1999).
- A decision to make group work.

Sources for Vocabulary

- Experiences and images of the extreme sport of freefall: disorientation in sense of time/space spatial freedom/restriction specific gestures and physical aspects of falling speed anxiety.
- Quotations of movement from *Fix.*
- Film: use of real time – pauses.
- Traditional Kathak movements.
- Exploration of speed.
- Indian time cycle of $9\frac{1}{2}$ beats.

Style

- Contemporary Kathak; some naturalistic pedestrian movement; some percussive actions.
- Abstract; formalist but also allusive treatment of the theme.
- Collaborative approach producing integrated effect.
- Similar material shared equally between male and female dancers.
- Mathematical, complex structures allow dancers to drop into and out of unison unexpectedly, creates complex visual rhythms.
- Strong use made of repetition and variation. Splices material together in recombination; diminishment; accumulation; recycling.
- Strong use made of contrasts – speed, proximity, level, direction, flow.
- Rondo-like structures and approaches used.

Key Characteristics and Movements

- Downward focus.
- Little close proximity; no physical contact; structural/formal relationships between dancers.
- Spatial restriction; triangular formations; diagonal and straight lines, some curving pathways.
- Direct/precise (slicing, piercing, pressing, jabbing, rebounding, swaying); indirect/flexible use of space (flickering, fluttering, serpentine, scything, rippling); gestures often highlighted by incisive arrival; extreme speed and near stillness.
- Strong, sharp, heavy, relaxed, gliding, hovering, fluid, strobe-like/robotic qualities. Impetus/energy: dissipates; rebounds; transfers to another body part; or is suddenly arrested.
- Torso: flexed forward at hips with flat back; upright; occasionally with slight arch backwards.
- Leg gestures: deep knee bends, parallel and turn out; standing with heels together, in slight turnout; leg raised in front, parallel, knee flexed; high leg extensions to front and rear; low level circular kicks; scissor kicks with elevation (hitch-kick); lunges; kneeling.
- Feet: infrequent use of demi-point (rise onto balls of feet); foot often flat against the floor, raised foot is often relaxed; foot slaps floor with percussive sound; occasional flexed foot; ball of foot taps floor before stepping.
- Travelling: walk, run; ball-change step; spins/pivots; falling and rolls across floor; lunges; low level sliding; variety of hops and two-footed elevations; hand stand backwards/sideways; some off-balance.
- Arm gestures: variety of circles, smaller arcs and swings; curved overhead; extend sideways from shoulder in linear, wing-like shapes; hang parallel straight downwards to the floor; weaving around each other; flexed elbows; rock from side to side with hands in contact; flex in a small two-dimensional square shape, palms flat as if pushing a door; various Kathak positions; contacting head; different surfaces/parts contact floor; varieties of V shapes – splay outwards in a relaxed open shape which frames head (freefall image), also downward and backward directed V. Arms often propel/lead/help body into movement or arrest it, gesture is not just decorative.
- Hands: wrists flex and contact; palms and fingertips touch; hands flick and flutter;

hands drop heavily to contact side of thigh or slap floor with sound; support body weight; contact various body parts – head, knee, back of shoulders; tip of index finger and thumb press together, other fingers fan outwards; soft fists; quick rotations of wrist/lower arm with fist; wrists roll around each other; uncurling fingers; thumb pressed into side of palm; fingers interlocked/grasped overhead.

- Isolations: shoulder presses/rotates forward; head drops; quick successive joint flexion in arms.

Structural Overview Chart: a broad outline of *Rush*
Key: AK – Akram Khan; MM – Moya Michael; IP – Inn Pang Ooi.

PART 1

Section	Dance Material	Lighting
Entry	Pedestrian quality. Walking. Stand downstage, facing upstage with backs to audience. Long pause. Change stage position twice – stand in arrow head/triangular formations.	Lights slowly up – dim, white. It silhouettes the dancers, slowly fades to blackout with crescendo in music. Brief flash of blue light and blackout.
Section 1	On the spot. Spatial restriction. Distinctive use of torso – flexed forward at hips. Circular arm gestures are key. Variety of hand embellishments (for example, flexed wrists, palms touching). Shoulder initiates occasionally. Dynamic qualities: sharp; sudden; rebounding; percussive; heavy; smooth; gliding; some light tension. Focus – often down; can follow arm gestures. Isolations – head drops backwards. Unison and canon: changes in pace, variations, reorganising of material brings each dancer into and out of unison with each of the others. 3 pauses (tableaux) in different positions (arms: outstretched sideways; reaching downwards; wide, square arms). Begins with dancers standing in new position (a Kathak pose); stillness (as opening of section 1).	Stage is dark except for two horizontal, curved strips of white light. Within the centre of the upstage one is MM; IP and AK are within the downstage one.
Section 2	Dancers call out boles. Begin to travel sideways and change level along the strips of light. Triangular formation retained. Different body parts initiate quick changes of direction.	Maintains section 1 strips of light.

Section	Dance Material	Lighting
	Dynamic qualities as section 1 with very fast floor phrases (remains similar throughout rest of dance). End of section is more gentle and slow.	
	Unison and canon as section 1. Some inclusion of material from section 1 within distinct phrases of new action content. Repetition; variation by changing ordering of actions. Brief quotations from *Fix*.	
	Pauses briefer than section 1 and tableaux not always in identical pose; new Kathak poses; one long tableau with flooding light (arms extended straight in front, palms contacting) suddenly fling backwards, snapping apart.	Long pause – strong blue light floods from down-stage lamps. Then quickly off as arms snap. The strips slowly fade and the whole floor is now dim white.
	Slow walking in linear pathways at end of section to new stage placement. Ends with dancers at low level, sitting on heels, arms snap open in repeat.	
Section 3	Duet: IP and MM. AK placed apart, kneeling upstage left, watches. Includes: lengthy, strobe-like low level phrase; travelling sections with new high elevations and rolling across floor; longer quotations from Fix; curving and linear floor patterns, unison and canon.	Keeps dim white floor for duet. During the later travelling sections the floor changes to blue.
	Unison: AK rejoins fully with new floor sequence (sitting down backwards; sliding onto knees) that includes repeat of some MM and IP duet material and small ball-change steps (one arm spirals upwards to end vertically aloft) repeated facing different directions. (Ball-change – accented rhythm, two quick/small alternating steps, on the spot).	
	Repeat long tableau gesture from section 2 but no pause or snap open this time. Head initiates run to new stage placement – a diagonal line. Unison; new material (wrist to forehead, hitch-kick/elevation with backwards scissoring leg gestures) associated with repetition of low level material from opening of this section.	Brief tableau brings quick lighting changes – to darker blue then whiter again.

Section	Dance Material	
	Running to several new stage placements – but remaining briefly. Short repetition of duet relationship – this time MM watches.	
	Repeat gesture from long tableau from section 2 – slight pause. Followed by AK solo material (variations of previous material from all sections) while MM and IP unison (elbows drawn in and out repeatedly). All drop into brief unison then AK separate again.	
	Unison falling/floor material (includes tapping of hands behind head onto back of shoulders). Walk to repeat triangular stage placement. Repeat of tableau pose using 2 Kathak positions, trio not identical now. Repeat of early travelling material from this section (including quotations from *Fix*). Run forward to end downstage, facing upstage as opening of *Rush* (although MM is in AK's previous place). MM's arm drops and signals blackout.	At end of Part 1 fast fade then sudden blackout.
PART 2 Section 1	MM placed upstage centre (as opening, Part 1). Solo; on the spot, repeated arm circling then arms extended, extreme speed and near stillness. AK in close proximity briefly.	Most of stage dark, dim white light focuses on MM.
Section 2	IP walks into column and sudden static, unison; as Part 1, repetition, variation, accumulation develops the simple components (arm circles, lift of knee). Closer proximity; IP facing downstage right, AK/MM facing downstage left. Percussive foot action. AK uses variations in action/pace to drop into, and out of, unison; also MM later. Canon develops, static Kathak gesture (arm extends diagonally, palm upwards, fingers uncurl), short pause; longer pause in new tableau pose (stooping, elbow resting on bent knee).	Lights change quickly to three overlapping circles of pale blue light at stage centre (fleur-de-lys pattern).
	Travel sequence: repeat static Kathak gesture and stooping pose with stepping to new stage placement. Similar spatial relationship: IP still facing downstage, AK/MM upstage left, diagonal line. Variations on static unison material above with material from Part 1 Section 2 gradually included (sitting on heels).	

Section	Dance Material	Lighting
	Begin to move more freely around the stage. Repeated stepping/pausing pattern (large steps into new pose – lunge, torso flexed forward, arms bent in front, hands in soft fist shape) to make new stage placements and arrive in triangle formation with MM upstage centre again. Continue to explore variations on the opening arm circling, unison material interspersed with actions from the stepping pattern just performed.	Overlapping circles disappear – white floor.
	Repeat stepping/pausing pattern above. Maintain spatial distance and two versus one relationship. Dropping into and out of unison (two in unison, one different). Begin to add repetition of low level material from Part 1 (kneeling, elbow placed on floor) with new material (IP handstand variation with leg extending low backwards).	
	AK briefly walks upstage left to watch MM and IP who perform more extensive travelling, repetitions of previous material and a new low level pose in which AK finally joins (kneeling, one leg fully extended behind, arms straight supporting upright Sphinx-like torso).	
	Linear formation across the stage. Distinctive flexed torso Part 1, Section 1, and standing upright; simple V shaped arm gestures embellished by hand flicks or heavy, larger lower arm flicks; small steps backwards, travel upstage.	Floor blue. Two rows of paler oval lights; downstage row fades as trio move upstage.
Section 3	Solo – MM. Includes variations on previous material (knee lifts), new material (high leg gesture in front and behind, large elevation with legs in tucked position). AK and IP watch.	MM solo – lights brighter, though ovals still visible.
	Brief solo• – AK. Mainly gestural: includes new material (hands drawn close to side of head; arm raised at side of head with flexed elbow and wrist).	

Section	Dance Material	Lighting
	Complex changing relationships and recycling of material builds great energy for the remainder of this section:	
	MM unison with IP, then AK with IP, using variations of her solo material (high leg behind is carried to side; repeat of tucked jump). MM introduces variations from previous material including quick changes of level (sphinx-like kneeling). Brief unison with repeat of ball-change component, then MM another brief solo – repeat of earlier travelling phrase (run, balance, torso ripple).	
	Trio walk to meet centre stage briefly (as in opening of part 2, section two) and on to new stage placement. Remain for brief repetition of low level phrase.	
	Facing upstage then basic Kathak pose (both elbows flexed) repeated in three different directions.	
	AK/MM simultaneous solo: AK exact repeat of brief solo• above; MM repeats linear stepping/turning pattern from part 1, section 2. IP is motionless. AK in brief complementary unison with MM. Trio then perform simple arm swinging gesture.	Ovals slowly disappear – floor white.
	AK uses different travel pattern to IP and MM. All end downstage right and IP suddenly changes direction with turning elevation. AK and MM unison – includes recycling and variations of part 1 material (quotations from Fix). IP joins them. Mostly unison.	
	Travel upstage: simple, repeated phrase (sitting on heels and rebounding). Then coalesce towards downstage left and repeat part of static, arm circling sequence from opening of Part 2, section 2. Sequence continues briefly after music stops. Trio clasp raised knees. Ends abruptly.	Sudden blackout.

Analysing *Rush*: ideas for practical and theoretical tasks

Teacher's Note: there are further resources listed that will need to be collected for some of the tasks. Read through the text first before beginning any of the tasks. Music to accompany practical work is not suggested here. There is no shortage of classical, modern fusion or Bollywood style music available. The tasks are divided according to different aspects of *Rush*. The teacher should decide how to divide the study between AS and A2 courses. The latter involves a key focus on the wider context but it is important to cover enough of this for AS to support an appropriate understanding and enjoyment of the work. Practical tasks explore Khan's work in a creative manner to develop choreographic experience and other aspects of the course as well as elucidate *Rush*.

Starting Points and Sources for Vocabulary

Khan uses the experience and images from freefall:

Find illustrations or descriptions of freefalling. A useful website is http://skydiving.skydivewww.com. Use these positions to create action phrases – include some static work. Experiment with not being upright.

Imagine you are tumbling out of an aircraft. Start at one end of the room on the floor and explore ways of rolling across the floor as if you were tumbling slowly through the air, try to place as many of the surfaces of the body and limbs as possible in contact with the floor at some point. Repeat the task with one dancer walking by the side (not too close) of the tumbling/rolling dancer. Whenever they see an interesting body position they should call out 'now'. The performer tries to pause or sway in this position.

Find a feather (or make some paper aeroplanes) or any item that will fly through the air in an indirect manner. Watch the trajectory of its fall. Record this and use it to create a track for limbs to describe or particular joints to descend through.

Khan explores different energy flows:
Use the above tasks to define a sequence of rolling and pausing. Perform it fluidly first. Now experiment with using a sudden and successive, strobe-like quality instead.

Explore and find actions using descriptive words for energy flow – for example: explode; rebound; ripple; and compress.

Khan experiments with speed:
Take any movement and see how fast it can be made to go. Notice how greater speed needs increased stability at the base of support or a lower centre of gravity if travelling.

Improvise using Khan's instructions to his dancers (see Part 3). He describes how different parts become heavy and begin to fall.

Khan uses different body parts to initiate action:
Explore how different body parts can lead an action, for example a simple run in the opposite direction can be initiated by the head dropping, circling around and the body has to follow. This same change of direction can be led by a shoulder or a knee.

Khan draws circles with a variety of body parts too. Look at the notation symbols for different body parts.

Structuring Methods

Khan makes use of the contrast between central and peripheral transitions when directing arm gestures into different directions:
The arm may arc in a semicircle or flex and draw into the centre of the body before extending. Notate an arm circle and explore the possible directions. Create a short phrase (sequence A) that explores central and peripheral transitions between four of the directions. You could choose a phrase length that does not use an easy 4 count pattern, try an odd number such as 7, 9 or 13. This will give at least some experience of the asymmetry of the Indian time cycle Khan uses. Or make an 8 count phrase first then explore what happens to it when the same movements are counted as a 7, 9 or 13 count phrase.

Khan recombines short sections from his phrases and uses unison:

In small groups (of two or three) use the phrase created in the above task. Join them together to make a longer sequence (sequence B).

Decide on some new material (from the warm up of the lesson for example). Recombine sequence A and mix with the new material to make sequence C. Perform Sequences B and C one after the other in unison.

Khan generates variations from simple components:

Use the short phrase (sequence A) from the first task above. Add: a hand embellishment; a direction change; a change of pace; put the movement into a different body part; travel with a change of level to make sequence D.

Khan uses a variety of relationships in his trio but two dancers moving in unison while one performs individual material, or works in canon, is most typical:

In small groups use the phrases developed above to explore this relationship. For example, a trio perform sequence B in unison, then one dancer performs sequence C while the other two perform D.

Now interject some material from sequence D into B. Perform the phrases again to see how canons can be made by this effect.

Khan makes use of recombination, repetition and variation:

Explore other choreographers using similar methods of recombination/variation to broaden the choreographic experience of students. For example, works by Shobana Jeyasingh, Richard Alston, Siobhan Davies, Lea Anderson, Wayne McGregor.

Khan uses spatial restriction:

Works by Lea Anderson and Russell Maliphant also employ this. Make a travelling sequence based on repertoire examples chosen from *Rush*. Use the gestures but restrict the material to the spot; or employ the fullest performance possible of the sequence but restrict it to low levels, each gesture involving a separate weight transference across the ground.

Khan uses chance based processes or stands outside and organises material:

Take sequence B or C created above and arrange this to interlock across several bodies like Khan does in his columns – use an outside eye and decide the order/pace on the basis of what it looks like. Take sequence D and use a chance-based process to create pauses at different moments for different dancers (for example, throw a dice three times – to determine a count that the pause will begin on, the bar it will happen in and the number of counts it will last).

Khan is influenced by film and describes his work as cinematic:

Two dancers can improvise a movement conversation using material created for sequence A. Pauses should be interjected in the movement and can be held for as long as dancers feel it is 'real'.

Use the words 'cut', 'splice', 'freeze frame', and 'rewind' to create a new sequence.

Khan uses quotations from *Fix*: To explore this repertory the video of this work (details in Part 2) needs to be obtained or see the description in Part 3: the Choreography.

Fix a joint or body part in space and explore how the body can move around this fixed point. Look at how notation is used to record this concept.

Khan can 'arch, dip and spiral with extravagant grace' (Mackrell 2001):

Use these movement words to create your own phrase.

Look at the anatomy of the spine.

Kathak

Arrange a professional workshop or use the video *Siksha Kathak* (see Section 2 for contact details). It is not necessary however to be able to perform Kathak to study *Rush* (see appendix 6: dancers biographies). A taster would be enough. However, experimenting with the movement concepts would be useful. See the tasks below.

Clap 4, then 8 then 16 beats taking the same amount of time so the speed doubles each time. Try this with simple stepping too. Clap the trital rhythm given in Part 2. Divide the class into two groups to clap Andy Cowton's rhythmic pattern in Part 3.

Take a very simple stepping pattern, for example, three steps on the spot and heel placed out to the side with bent supporting leg. Begin slowly then double the time as for clapping task above to experience the three speeds described in section 2. Create simple stepping patterns to beat/step onto different parts of feet. For example: extend right leg in front and step onto the heel (foot is flexed up), replace the weight onto the left foot, step again on right foot next to it, (rhythm is '1 and 2); or place ball of foot across the support, extend it out and place heel down with partial weight-bearing, then close feet (it has nearly the same rhythm, 1 and a 2'). See how many variations of steps to these rhythms can be created.

Clap and then speak a simple rhythm. It is not necessary to use boles just experience speaking the counts out loud. Students now find steps to mimic this pattern.

Find ways of pivoting on a flat foot or with the toes slightly raised so weight is more into the heel, for example step, turn, step sideways or multiple turns on the spot, pushing off with the gesturing leg for each turn. The video *Siksha Kathak* gives examples that are simple to copy.

Tukra – short phrases of 6 or 7 bars at the end of which the dancer take a typical Kathak pose and holds it for 1 bar. Perform some of the simple stepping patterns from the above tasks for 4 bars, use spins for bars 5- 6 and arrive in a flourish on the first beat of bar 7 and hold this (make up your own position, choose from the video Siksha Kathakor, or any photographs you might have for example, the front cover of *Dancing Times*, September 1995).

Notate the simple Kathak poses described in Section 2 (these are used in *Rush*). Use them in the tukra created above.

Photographic Task

See photograph on page 59 (rehearsal photograph from company archive).
Identify the section and phrase that the photograph illustrates. Where else does similar material/variations occur? How does the body shape link to the starting points? Notate the illustration. Explore: the anatomical structure of the spine and hip; technique and safe practice involved; exercises to develop core stability and strength; exercises to develop

flexibility in the hamstrings. Reconstruct some of the action material that surrounds the position in the photograph. How might this material reflect the starting points and theme? Find your own variations using this material.

Information and Communication Technology

View a video clip of Khan's *Loose in Flight* on the CD-Rom *Living Tradition* (2000) listed in Key Visual Resources in Part 2: Background contexts. The following comments indicate what can be seen there. Khan has: a 'dazzling mixture of macho foot speed and honeyed muscular tone' (Brown 2002); a 'lyrically generous upper body ... commanding, graceful and charismatic, [and] a blistering percussive attack' (Craine 2001). The quotations by Brown and Craine can be used as the basis for a discussion or an essay, are they still pertinent as a description of *Rush*? Experiment with Khan's starting points for *Loose in Flight* (see Part 1: The Creators) and reconstruct some of the vocabulary illustrated.

Research the people listed as influences on Khan. See Part 1: The Creators and also Appendix 2: Influences on Akram Khan. A useful source of dance information is the CD-ROM: *Dance Current Awareness Bulletin* listed under Part 2, key visual resources. How do these influences appear to have affected Khan's work and approaches? In particular it will be noticed that there are few British names. Why might this be?

Research the South Asian dance context within the UK. See Part 2: lists useful websites and CD-ROMs. For example, use DCAB: search for articles on Birju Maharaj; names of choreographers working within different styles within the UK; information regarding funding/philosophy or discussions regarding the tradition versus the modern. Each article found has a brief summary and can be purchased from the National Resource Centre for Dance for further reference.   Use *Living Tradition* for illustrations and video clips. It also provides a database of UK performers and contacts.

Find illustrations of Indian art and sculptures of Nataraja: try www.thebritishmuseum.ac.uk; www.dm-art.org; as starting points. The National Museum of India website, www.nationalmuseumindia,org, is a good source too but the illustrations are rather small. www.asiasocietymuseum.com has video clips on Shiva and a time line. www.vam.ac.uk, the website of the Victoria and Albert Museum in London, has an introduction to the Nehru Gallery of Indian Art. Local libraries are also a good source of Hindu art books – there are many to choose.

Traditional costume design can be seen in 17th and 18th century miniature painting. The Metropolitan Museum of Fine Art in Boston has a good collection some of which are currently reproduced in birthday cards published by Canns Down Press (see www.cannsdownpress.co.uk for local stockists).

www.pratappawar.com has photographs of Kahn as a young dancer, pictures of Pratap Pawar and Birju Maharaj.

Making an analysis

The AQA GCE AS/A Level Dance Specification requires students to be able to 'comment perceptively and critically on the structural and expressive aspects of dance'. Key to this is having access to an analytical process suitable for GCSE AS/A level that helps students to identify the salient features in order that interpretations made can be based upon evidence. Students often express unsupported opinions relying on personal prejudice when they first engage in analytical thinking and are unable to explain the reasons why they hold particular views. The first step is to enable students to perceive and describe the constituent features of the dance and their interrelationships (for example, actions, dynamic qualities, use of space, structuring methods, design elements). This involves developing descriptive language and may also take the form of notation to record movement evidence.

Students sometimes find it difficult to progress beyond a basic narration of the dance. After gathering the evidence interpretations can be made. Interpretations are supported opinions about the meanings and effects of the elements. Some knowledge of the wider context will be necessary. It is not possible usually to make articulate interpretations without some understanding of the genre and style involved. Students should explain their interpretations using evidence from the work. This requires a more sophisticated response than simple description and is expected within Unit 3 of the AS examination. The final step entails evaluation when an understanding of the significance of a work and its effects within the wider dance context is demonstrated. Some response at this level may be necessary at Unit 3 but is a requirement for Unit 6 of the A2 examination. Students should explain their evaluations drawing on a range of information from the artistic, historical and cultural context. This analytical process should assist in successful study at GCE AS/A Level Dance by providing a fuller understanding of the work. Importantly, it will also give students a greater sense of enjoyment of the dance.

Individual teachers should use their own judgment about the depth of study required at AS and A level. New teachers should refer to the AQA Specification. An integrated approach to teaching and learning is suggested. Although the practical tasks are written separately, it is for the teacher to determine when they should support theoretical study.

Using the Structural Overview Chart and Analysis Summary

Musically *Rush* is divided into two parts, within which it is possible to section the material in different ways. One could attend to lighting changes, the introduction of new action content, shifts in the structuring methods, or pauses. Each one of these provides a sense of order but none has dominance. The Structural Overview Chart (SOC) gives this author's interpretation. It is provided for ease of identifying a simple outline so that when writing about *Rush* students can clarify where in the dance examples might be found. A detailed analysis that expands on this skeletal outline must be undertaken. Each point on the SOC should be identified and a full description of it pursued by observing the video. Students must be encouraged to form their own opinions and to gather detailed evidence. A simple rote learning of the SCO would not be sufficient in answer to GCE A level examination questions. Music is not included in the SCO. This is so that students can add their own column to describe changes in this. An Analysis Summary provides a list of the key characteristics and helps to identify movement content for students when undertaking the detailed analysis.

Teacher's Note:

- There are two recordings of *Rush* on the video. The second version gives clarity as to floor pattern but the first version gives a clearer view of the detail of the movement. It might be useful to refer to this version when making a detailed analysis and fill in missing details from the second version. Differences between the two and the impact on any interpretations made can be discussed.

- Students should keep floor plans, notation, diagrams/pin men drawings and full notes. It is helpful to record which dancer is which using a code (see the SOC).

- The first task for the beginning of every section is to draw a floor plan of where the dancers are placed and their facing. Changes in stage placement (indicated in the SOC), pathways of travel and the end of every section should also be documented.

• Teachers may find it convenient, although it is not essential, to use a proforma for collecting evidence (with sections for action content; use of space; dynamics; structural relationships; design and audio effects; and interpretations). This will help to bring order to the students' notes. Colours could also be used to highlight particular events/people within the notes for ease of reference.

• A working knowledge of the starting points and context will be required before a detailed analysis is undertaken.

• Read Part 3 and look for evidence in the work.

• Key: AK – Akram Khan; MM – Moya Michael; IP – Inn Pang Ooi.

Important: The questions below are not exhaustive and are offered to encourage a spirit of enquiry. The aim is to expand upon the statements in the SCO, to provide tools for analysis and guidance so that students can form their own interpretations. Refer to SOC to see where each section begins and ends.

Part 1
Entry
Draw a floor plan and note entrances and placement of dancers. Notate the two changes of stage placement. Describe the lighting and the music. What effect is created by the use of stillness and a tableau? (Tableau – a term used here to identify the static arrangements of bodies in linear or triangular stage placements) What is the impact of the lighting and music? How does it relate to the theme of the dance? What expectations are set up?

Section 1
How is the opening of this section spatially restricted and what dynamic qualities are used? What is the effect of this? Watch each dancer in turn perform the simple opening circular movements. Who does which movements and when? How are pauses used? How do they get into unison? How is the torso used? Where is the general focus? What is the effect of the use of such simple movements?

A new phrase of material is now introduced by IP. What is it? What new material is MM performing? At what point does she pick up on IP's material? How many ways does the use of the hand embellish the movement and make contact? Note how AK recombines IP and MM's new material. Look at the categories of actions in both new phrases – both have hands in contact and include a rocking motif for example They end this new phrase in unison with torso upright and hands splayed in a relaxed V to the side of the head. What is the significance of this body shape? Why is there a gentle swaying?

What happens to the use of focus in this section? What dynamic qualities are used? How phrases interlock and repeat across the group will be important throughout the whole of the work. Look at how it constructs a visual rhythm.

Is it possible to discern a time cycle of $9\frac{1}{2}$ beats? If not, why not? What effect might the time cycle have on the rhythm of the movement? It is very difficult for non-Kathak trained dancers to discern complex time cycles. Do not worry if it is not visible. The music gives no pulse so the dancers are not moving in rhythmical relationship to it. However, it might be seen to give an asymmetrical, complex feeling to the phrases. Khan refers to the need to reproduce a sense of anxiety.

Note all moments of stillness. What is the relationship between these in terms of body shape? How does these shapes/stillness relate to the theme? Look at what new material is introduced later in the section. What old material is combined into this new material? Look for repeats and who is performing when. All arrive finally in similar Kathak position (one arm extended sideways at shoulder height, the other bent in front). This is the third tableau pause and forms a transition to the next section.

Summarise the effects of this section – for example, what is the impact of spatial restriction, the use of pauses, use of dynamic qualities, use of repetition? How is it structured into short phrases? What is the effect of the lights? What is the effect of the non-pulse based music? How does it create difficulties for the dancers? The manner of repetition and introduction of new material is typical of the whole dance and is key to the mathematical precision in the structuring, reordering and combining of components. A detailed noting of who is moving and when is essential. How does this all link to the theme?

Section 2

How does the use of stillness relate to the beginning phrase of section 1? The dancers call out boles. Why? What is the effect of hearing these? The dancers begin to travel sideways: what movements are used, what is the impact after the previous spatial restriction? Look at how direction changes are initiated. How do the arms lead and propel? What is the effect of the lighting on this travelling? In what order do the dancers move? What is the effect of the floor work? How does it link to the theme? Look at the new material. For example, stepping and turning, arms alternating like pistons. Describe the phrase that employs this. There are several actions that might be evocative of freefalling and parachuting? Some of this material is taken from *Fix*. Look at the manner in which speed operates.

What material is repeated from Section 1? Look at how it is structured and reordered. Note new material and specific Kathak gestures – use the Analysis Summary. Look at the tableaux. How does the treatment differ to previous ones? Look at the lighting effect during the longest pause (a key moment). What is the effect? How is the tableau evocative of freefall?

Look at the dynamic qualities? Are they the same throughout? What is the effect of this?

Summarise the effects of this section – as for section 1. Also look at relationships and contrasts between sections 1 and 2.

Section 3

What is the effect of AK watching the opening duet? Identify the material, dynamics and use of space for this duet. Look at the strange effect of the successive body action in the floor section. This is what Khan refers to as 'hovering' quality. Note other repeats of this relationship – one dancer watching the other two.

Look at how different perspectives are used – side views, back views. Look at how small components are repeated not just longer sections.

Identify new material introduced in this section. Note how old and new material mix together. There are further quotations from *Fix*. What happens to the floor patterns in this section? Look at the new use of a diagonal line – identify the material. Look at the increasingly complex exchanging of relationships – they drop into and out of unison with each other.

What happens to the tableau pauses? Why does the end of this section feel rondo-like?

Summarise the effects of this section: look at the way that spatial restriction gives way to freedom. Note how each section introduces new action content but reuses old material too. Note how speed increases over the part 1 of *Rush*. Make interpretations in respect of the theme of freefall – images, quality of movement, spatial distance maintained. How does Khan play with disorientation in sense of time and space felt during freefall? What is the overall effect of music and lighting?

Part 2
Section 1
How does the opening of this relate to Section 1 of Part 1? Link the action content to freefall. What is the impact of the lighting?

Section 2
Look at the action content for the opening column. How does it relate to material in part 1, Section 1? How is it developed? Look at how AK uses variations. A tableau is used again. How does this relate to part 1?

Look at the travelling sequences. How is new material introduced and what is its effect? Floor patterns become complex. The phrase using a stooped over position with both hands in a fist is what Khan's calls walking and nudging – the structure was created using chance.

Note the effect of this. How does it link to freefall?
Identify the new action content and how it is mixed with old material. There is more freedom to move around the stage. Look at the changes in stage placement, actions used and floor patterns created. What is the effect of this? The two versus one relationship between the dancers remains typical. Look how this is managed and the effect of its use.

Look at the ending material. How has it been prepared for in previous material? How is it evocative of freefall?

Summarise the effects of this section: look at how section 1 and 2 link together and their relationship to part 1. Look at the way that spatial restriction and freedom operates.

Section 3
The first solos begin to appear. What material is used? Look at the way that new material is still being introduced at this stage and the manner in which old material is recycled. Note how variations on movements continue to be created throughout.

Note the fast changes in relationships throughout the rest of this section. What material is being used, by whom and when? What is the effect of this? How is material recycled? Look at the use of unison and canon. What happens to the dynamic qualities in this section?

Tableaux effects are referred to. There is also some repetition by diminishment – simple components unpicked from longer sequences. Look at the rondo-like effect of the end. Summarise the effects of this section: look at how it relates to the previous two sections. Look at how the two halves of the dance relate to each other. Summarise the structuring methods. In particular:

• Link to freefall and other starting points.

• Note the effect of lighting, music and costume overall. In particular: read Part 3 and look for evidence of the impact of music and lighting; and refer to Part 2 for costume issues. How does Khan's costume design relate to traditional choices for Kathak performances? There are two useful books to give a background in lighting issues both available from Dance Books (www.dancebooks.co.uk): *The Dance Experience*, edited by M.H Nadel and M. R. Strauss, published by Princetown (2003) has an article by lighting designer Rick Yeatman on the history of the craft; and *The Stage Lighting Handbook*, by F. Reid, (2001) for practical issues.

• Look at how the dance material uses and develops Kathak approaches (refer to Part 2) although not many actual Kathak actions are performed.

• Identify possible influences from choreographers admired by Khan (see Appendix 2).

Appendix 1

Shiva's Cosmic Dance: the divine origins of dance

(Source: Khokar, M., The Splendours of Indian Dance, New Delhi: Himalayan Books, 1988.)

In Hindu mythology dance and drama are god-given activities. Brahmā is the first deity in the Hindu Trinity. Vishnu is the second deity; he is the preserver of mankind and has a merciful aspect. Krishna is an incarnation of Vishnu. Śiva (pronounced Shiva) is the third deity. He is the origin of cosmic movement and in his aspect as Nataraja, the Lord of the Dance, he is considered to be both creator and destroyer in a cyclical process. At the centre of the Universe, in a golden hall, Śiva performed the original tandava dance to all of the gods. Movements (karanas) from this are celebrated in temple sculptures and were danced by the devadesi temple dancers. There are also well known bronze statues of Śiva in his iconographic pose as Nataraja in which he is depicted with four arms within a halo of fire. One hand holds a drum from which the sound produces a new cycle of creation, another holds a ball of fire which signifies destruction, a palm is raised in a gesture of protection (abhaya) and another points to his foot (gaja hasta) which tells of the path to salvation. He stands on the dwarf of ignorance and his raised foot gives release from bondage.

Indra asked Brahmā to suggest a pastime worthy of the gods because they were bored and he created drama (Natya) writing the details in the Natya Veda, the sacred book. Bharāta Muni was asked to produce the first drama for the delectation of the gods. Although all were pleased by the performance, Śiva thought that there was not enough dancing in it and so he taught his tandava dance to Bharāta who then incorporated it into his treatise, the Natyasastra. Tandava is a vigorous style of dance but lasya was danced later by Śiva's consort Parvati, and hence is delicate and gentle.

Appendix 2

Influences on Akram Khan

Theatre/Film

Kathak

Modern Dance

Sir Peter Brook
Khan performed in his
Adventures of Mowgli and
Hamlet.

Birju Maharaj
The teacher of Khan's
teacher and a direct link
to the celebrated
Lucknow school.

Jonathan Burrows
A key early influence.
Khan made a duet with
him.

Ang Lee
Wong Kai-Wai
Khan admires their films.

Akram Khan

Alain Platel
Siddi Larbi
Khan admires their
company, Les Ballets C
de la B and plans to work
with Larbi.

Satyajit Ray
David Lynch
Khan admires their ability
to use 'real' time within
films.

Pratap Pawar
Khan is his disciple.

Saburo Teshigawara
Emile Greco
Pina Bausch
Trisha Brown
William Forsythe
Khan admires their work.

Appendix 3: Touring Schedule of *Rush*

(reproduced with permission from Akram Khan Company, compiled by Cecilia Fogado)

	DATE	VENUE	COUNTRY
2000	20 – 22 July	Rosas Performance Space	Brussels
		Programme: *Fix*; *Rush* (work in progress)	

Tour of *Rush* on programme which included *Fix* and *Loose in Flight* (as film version, but occasionally as stage version)

	DATE	VENUE	COUNTRY
	5 Oct	Midland Arts Centre, Birmingham (première)	UK
	7 Oct	Norwich Playhouse	UK
	12-13 Oct	Green Room, Manchester	UK
	18 Oct	Acorn Theatre, Penzance	UK
	20 Oct	Danse a Lille	France
	22 Oct	Romaeuropa Festival	Italy
	26 – 28 Oct	Lilian Baylis Theatre, London Dance Umbrella Festival.	UK
	3 Nov	Dome Theatre, Brighton	UK
	10 Nov	Swindon Town Hall Studios	UK
	15 Nov	Surrey University, Guildford	UK
	18 Nov	Riley Theatre, Leeds	UK
	24 Nov	Derby Dance Centre	UK
2001	31 Jan -1 Feb	Laban Centre, London	UK
	7 Feb	Cultural Centre Berchem, Antwerp	Belgium
	13 Feb	Nuffield Theatre, Lancaster	UK
	15 Feb	Unity Theatre, Liverpool	UK
	23-24 Feb	Dundee	UK
	3-4 March	Bremen	Germany
	9-25 March	Johannesburg and Durban	South Africa
	13-15 April	Berlin	Germany
	21- 22 April	Springdance Festival, Utrecht	Netherlands
	27-28 April	Tramway, Glasgow	UK
	4 May	Arnolfini, Bristol	UK
	5 May	Norwich Playhouse	UK
	9 May	unknown	Estonia
	11 May	Bratislava	Czechoslovakia
	29 May	Jerusalem	Israel
	1-2 June	Tel Aviv	Israel
	16 June	Uzes	France
	14-15 July	Kalamata Festival	Greece
	24 July	Full Moon Festival	Finland
	26-29 July	Vienna	Austria
	13-14 Sept	Jacarta	Indonesia
	19-23 Sept	Columbia	Argentina
	16-29 Sept	Buenos Aires	Argentina
	8-9 Oct	Paris	France
	18-21 Oct	Columbus, Ohio	USA
	24-27 Oct	The Kitchen, New York	USA
	29 Oct-3 Nov	Vancouver East Cultural Centre	Canada
	5-6 Nov	Ottawa	Canada
	14-16 Dec	Creteil	France
2002	May	International Festival	Ireland
	29 Oct	Queen Elizabeth Hall, London	UK
	29-30 Nov	Teatre de la Ville, Paris	France

Appendix 4

Biographies of dancers

(source: Akram Khan Company archives)

Gwyn Emberton

Gwyn Emberton graduated from Middlesex University with a BA (Hons) in dance performance in 1999. During this time he was a member of the National Youth Dance Company for two years, touring in the UK and Europe. After graduating he worked with Janet Smith's Scottish Dance Theatre performing in works by Smith and Jan De Shynkel. He has also taught for the Scottish School of Contemporary Dance and Middlesex University. He joined Akram Kahn after touring Europe with Adventures in Motion Pictures in their production of Matthew Bourne's *Swan Lake*.

Moya Michael

Moya Michael was born in Johannesburg, South Africa. As a dance student at the Technikon in Pretoria she created two works *Unplugged* and *Tish and Jo* that were performed in the annual Dance Umbrella in Johannesburg. In 1998 she created *Ten versus 45:15* for the State Theatre Dance Company which was sponsored by the Royal Netherlands Embassy. In 1998 she received a scholarship for PARTS in Brussels. Under the direction of Anne Teresa De Keersmaeker she has studied the repertoire of Rosas, Trisha Brown, William Forsythe. She has also worked with choreographers Jonathan Burrows and Thomas Hauert (Switzerland). She has performed with Vuyani Dance Theatre at the Springdance Festival, Holland. She joined Akram Kahn researching material for *Rush*. In July 2000 she was nominated for an Outstanding Dancer Award at the international theatre school festival in Amsterdam, Holland. In 2003 she performed her own choreography Hatch, in the Purcell Room, South Bank Centre, London with Shannell Winlock (Akram Khan Company) and Maho Ihara (Retina and the Cholmondeleys).

Inn Pang Ooi

Inn Pang Ooi obtained a scholarship to train at The Hong Kong Academy for Performing Arts and was a member of Transitions Dance Company in 2000. He has worked with various companies and choreographers in Hong Kong, Japan, Taiwan, Austria and the UK, including Rosalind Newman, Kei Takei, Hwai-min Lin, Ismeal Ivo, Marcia Haydée, Kerry Nicholls and Filip van Huffel. He joined Akram Khan Company in 2001.

Appendix 5

Resource materials: extracts from reviews

'As with many arresting dancers, his problem as a choreographer has been that of making dance on bodies that aren't his own. Khan can't help but be an attention magnet, which damages the trio *Rush*... Cowton's.... uncomfortable sandpaper score... flicks your ear drums, and with cold lighting and formal patterns to keep us at bay.'
David Jays, 'Dance Umbrella 2002', *Dancing Times*, January 2003, p.45.

'consolidating charisma into a language with two other dancers, who, to their credit, are hot on his heels with dexterity and whip-cracking force. An elemental, ship's engine of a soundtrack is the driving force for this study into the knife-edge between hovering stillness and mesmerising velocity... using the body to draw polyrhythms in space... the dancers' arms splice the air, like a windfarm in a gale they move always in precise constellations.'
Catherine Hale, Akram Khan, magazine section, November 2002, www.ballet.co.uk

'he takes motifs from *Fix* – spins, falls and rolls – and formalises them into rhythmic patterns. At first you watch only him, then the structure takes over.'
Jan Parry, 'He flies through the air with the greatest of ease', *Sunday Observer*, 29 October 2000 (no page available)

'the free-fall experienced by paragliders before they pull the parachute cord... fast, angular and tightly patterned choreography... the emphasis was on arms as wings, propellers and pendulums. The piece was beautifully abetted by... Cowton's rumbling, tingling sound track.'
Donald Hutera, 'British debut: a young choreographer impresses', *The Times*, section 2, 1 November 2000, p.1

'Khan explored the dynamics of flight, the three dancers... as jet planes complete with wingflaps, wind resistance and drag. The sonic rumbles and screeches of Andy Cowton's score made the image complete.'
Jenny Gilbert, 'Less is more when cultures clash on the dance floor,' *Independent on Sunday*, 4 February 2001, n.p.

Bibliography

Anonymous. *Classical and Folk Dances of India*, Bombay: Marg Publications. 1963

Anonymous. *Company Leaflet*, Performance at the University of Surrey, 15th November. 2000a

Anonymous. Critics' Circle Dance Awards 2000, www.sherringtons.co.uk/ceremony,htm, 29/11/02, 2000b

Anonymous. Akram Khan Extended Information, www.dance4.co.uk/Nottdance/akramext.html, accessed 29/11/02, 2002a

Anonymous. Akram rocks on. Pulse, 1, Spring, 2002b. p.4

Anonymous. *Art Works, ITV, 9th June*, ITV, 9.6.2002

Anonymous. Classical Turn. *southbank*, April, 2003a. p.6

Anonymous. Obituaries, Ram Gopal. *The Times*, p.31. October 14th, 2003b

Banerji, P. *Kathak Through the Ages*, New Delhi: Cosmo Publications. 1982

Banerji, S. S. *A Companion to Indian Music and Dance*, Delhi: Sri Satguru Publications. 1990

Bannerman, C. *South Asian Diaspora Dance in Britain*. SALIDAA (South Asian Diaspora Literature and Arts Archive), www.salida.org.uk, accessed 08/01/04.

Beaumont, C. *Michel Fokine and His Ballets*, London: C. W. Beaumont. 1945

Beaumont, C. *Complete Book of Ballets*, London: Putnam. 1949

Bhavnani, E. *The Dance in India*, Bombay: Taraporevala's Treasure House of Books. 1979

Bose, M. *Movement and Mimesis: the idea of dance in the Sanskritic Tradition*, Dordrecht/Boston/London: Kluwer Academic. 1991

Bragg, M. *South Bank Show, ITV, October*, ITV, October 2002

Brannigan, E. Maliphant: shaping space with bodies and light. At www.members.ozemail.co.au, accessed on 28/8/2001.

Brown, I. A star touched by his god, 27 November, www.telegraph.co.uk, accessed 27/11/02

Burrows, J. Leading Lights. *Dance Now*, 3, 1, Spring, 1994. pp.28 – 29

Coomaraswamy, A., K. *The Dance of Shiva*, New York:Dover. 1985

Craine, D. Dance: Akram Khan, Purcell Room. *The Times*, section 2, p.21. 11th April, 2001

De Marigny, C. lighting, realtime and Jennifer Tipton. *Dance Theatre Journal*, 11, 1, winter, 1993/94.

Ferguson, S. Akram Khan Company. *The Guardian*, www.guardian.co.uk, (accessed 08/01/04), 2000.

Frater, S. Triple-strength alliance. *Evening Standard*, p.40. Ist May, 2002

Hale, C. Akram Khan, October 2002, Queen Elizabeth Hall, November edition of Magazine at www.ballet.co.uk, accessed 26/11/2002

Hall, F., in B. Kansara (ed), *Academy of Indian Dance Seminar: the contribution of Indian Dance to British Culture*, Commonwealth Institute.1982,

Hutera, D. *Bringers of Light – Part Three*. www.worldwidedanceuk.com. accessed 12/01/2004

Iyer, A., Ed. *South Asian Dance: the British Experience*, Harwood Academic, Choreography and Dance: an International Journal. 1997

Jays, D. Spring Loaded '95. *Dancing Times*, June, 1995. p.895

Jays, D. Spring Loaded. *Dancing Times*, June, 1996. p.853.

Jordan, S. *Striding Out: Aspects of Contemporary and New Dance in Britain,* London: Dance Books. 1992

Kansara, B. (ed) Academy of Indian Dance Seminar. The contribution of Indian Dance to British Culture, Commonwealth Institute. 1982

Khan, A. Final Report to the Lisa Ullmann Travelling Scholarship Fund, Akram Khan Company Archive. 2000a

Khan, A. *Fix*, in Spring Re-Loaded Series 6, The Video Place. 2000b

Khan, A. in interview with Victoria Innes, www.londondance.com, 2002

Khan, A. in interview with Victoria Innes, Online Chat, www.londondance.com, accessed 07/01/03

Khan, A. personal communication with the author, 7th February, 2003

Khan, A. personal communication with the author, 27th February. 2004

Khan, A. Akram Khan: Choreographic Proposal. Akram Khan Company Archive. undated

Khokar, M. *Traditions of Indian Classical Dance*, London: Peter Owen. 1979

Khokar, M. *The Splendours of Indian Dance*, New Delhi: Himalayan Books. 1988

Kippen, J., and Bel, A. Lucknow Kathak Dance. article reprinted from *Bansuri,* Volume 13, 1996, www.pathcom.com/~ericp/kathak. accessed 08/01/04

Mackrell, J. *Out of Line: The Story of British New Dance*, London: Dance Books. 1992

Mackrell, J. The dazzling Akram Khan, April 10, www.guardian.co.uk, accessed 29/11/02 2002a

Mackrell, J. Related Rocks, December 11, www.guardian.co.uk, accessed 29/11/02 2002b

Mackrell, J. Kaash, May 13, www.guardian.co.uk, accessed 29/11/02 2002c

Mackrell, J. Legacy of Tradition. *The Guardian*, n.p. July 12, 2001

Massey, R. a. J. *Dances of India: a General Survey and Dancer's Guide,* London: Tricolour Books. 1989

Parry, J. He flies through the air with the greatest of ease. *The Observer*, page number not available. October 29th, 2000

Parry, J. First Class Air Male. *The Observer*, No page number available. May 6th, 2001

Parry, J. Let's get physics, May 19, www.observer.co.uk, accessed 27/11/02

Ramphal, V. Roots/Routes. *Dance Theatre Journal*, 18, 2, 2002. 16-19

Samson, L. *Rhythm in Joy: Classical Indian Dance Traditions*, India: Lustre Press. 1987

Sanders, L. Russell Maliphant. *Dancing Times*, February, 2002. pp.49-55

Sanders, L. interview with Andy Cowton, London, February 12th, 2004a

Sanders, L. Interview with Michael Hulls, 6th February, 2004b

Sanders, L. *Choreographer Fact Card: Shobana Jeyasingh*. National Resource Centre for Dance, 2004c

Smith, A. Reviews: New York City. *Dance Magazine*, Feb., 1998. p.100

Willis, M. Dancer in profile: Akram Khan. *Dancing Times*, March, 2001. pp.588-589